How About It?

Earl Wassom

Foreward By
Walt Brown, M.D.

Hello *Darkee*

THIS MOMENT PUBLISHERS®

4480 Georgetown/Greenville Road
Georgetown, IN 47122
812-951-3780
www.hellodarkee.com

Printed in the U.S.A.

10 9 8 7 6 5 4 3 2 1

ISBN 13: 978-0-9815475-0-3
ISBN 10: 0-9815475-0-8
Library of Congress Control Number: 2008901004

Scripture quotations identified as KJV are taken from the *King James Version* of the Bible.
Those identified as NKJV are taken from the *New King James Version,* ©1982 by Thomas Nelson, Inc. Used with permission. All rights reserved.
Scripture quotations identified NIV are taken from the Holy Bible, *New International Version,* ©1984 by International Bible Society. Used with permission of Zondervan. All rights reserved.
Scripture quotations identified NLT are from the Holy Bible, *New Living Translation,* ©1966. Used with permission of Tyndale House Publishers, Inc. All rights reserved.

Quote from Lt. General James Doolittle (p.16) used with permission.

Cover design by Donna Neely

About the Author

Earl Wassom is a native Oklahoman, born in 1923 and was attending college when World War II broke out. He enlisted in the Army Air Corp Aviation Cadet Program on August 9, 1942 and graduated as a Second Lieutenant Pilot on December 4, 1943 at Ellington Field, Texas. He received orders to B-24 Liberator bomber pilot transition school, Liberal, Kansas. He and his crew of nine other airmen trained together at Casper, Wyoming and were assigned overseas to the Eighth Air Force in Europe stationed at Attlebridge, England (station 120). With the 466th Bomb Group, he flew 35 missions into Germany and occupied Europe and eight additional missions into France hauling supplies to the gasoline deprived American ground forces. He completed his combat tour on March 18, 1945. He was awarded 5 Air Medals, the Purple Heart, and the Distinguished Unit Citation. He was reassigned to the Air Transport Command, Fifth Ferry Division and later, chose civilian life and was discharged in November 1945.

After the war, he was an active member in the Oklahoma Air National Guard. He continued his education and received a Doctorial degree in Education from Oklahoma State University. He felt that the universal need of mankind was spiritual in nature and prepared himself for the ministry and the field of education. He spent 12 years in the active ministry coupled with years of teaching in middle schools as a classroom teacher, basketball and football coach and vocal and instrumental music instructor. His doctoral degree awarded in 1967 prepared him for service in higher education. He served at Oklahoma State University and Western Kentucky University in the areas of instructional resources management, libraries, educational television, radio, museums and archives. His career included library consulting, both domestic and foreign. He retired in 1985 as Emeritus Professor, Western Kentucky University.

Following retirement, Wassom became actively engaged in the post-war Eighth Air Force Veteran's organizations. He has been a member of the Board of Directors of his own 466th Bomb Group; has served as Vice President, Executive Vice President, and President of the Second Air Division; and currently serves on the

Board of Directors of the Eighth Air Force Historical Society. He has been challenged to recruit membership and leadership for the Society from the next generation, children and grandchildren, to continue the legacy of the Veterans of the Eighth Air Force. During the past 15 years, he has served as Chaplain of the organization. He has published extensively in academic and military journals. He was co–author of his bomb group's history, *Attlebridge Arsenal* and was editor of the *Attlebridge Diaries with Supplement,* Second Edition.

Writing this book comes as a result of the promptings and desires of the Veterans of the Eighth Air Force to publish these essays which have been written by the Chaplain under the title, *How About It.* They have appeared over the past 15 years in the quarterly publications of the Society. The subject matter changes drastically from issue to issue and follows no set chronological pattern. These "pieces" have been written to "talk to the men" of The Mighty Eighth about overcoming the traumas of war experiences, the joy of peace, the issues of aging, the enjoyment of the fruits of surviving the war and their years of living. They have been written to encourage the men in their faith walk with God and to inspire the Spiritual life in all of us. The younger generation will be informed, enlightened and gain a better understanding of their predecessors as they read this book.

Table of Contents

Foreword

As a well-known historian and author of 8th Air Force volumes, Earl Wassom has produced a unique collection with themes not previously approached by other World War II authors. About fifteen years ago, Earl was contacted to see if he might write a regular column for *The Flyover* – the quarterly newsletter of the Tennessee Chapter of the 8th Air Force Historical Society. He called to discuss a proposal for his articles.

I was editor of that publication at the time and after hearing his ideas for contributions, I was convinced that Earl would be presenting an unusual and fresh approach to the history of the 8th Air Force's air war against Germany. His chosen title for the articles was *How About It!* The columns were an instant hit with the members of the Society. After I was named editor of the international *8th Air Force News* magazine, Earl agreed to continue writing his *How About It!* columns to be presented on the inside back cover of each issue. The idea was to close each issue with a thoughtful and inspiring piece for readers to take away. For over ten years, the members of the 8th AF Historical Society have been the appreciative recipients of articles that present a wide range of ideas and concepts from a writer who served in air combat during the most devastating war in history.

The columns in this volume, *Hello Darkee,* address major and minor aspects of the wartime era – 1942-1945. Each invariably ends with notes of inspiration, often with Biblical references that offer encouragement, understanding and hope for every reader. The experiences of this combat pilot are told in a manner of faith - faith in this life and faith in the one to follow.

Earl was twenty years old when he piloted a four-engine B-24 Liberator bomber with its ten-man crew. Missions were always accompanied by unpredictable combat actions on the way into targets of the German industrial complexes. Enemy fighters and ground-based anti-aircraft crews were formidable defenses against the bomber streams of the 8th Air Force flying from airbases in East Anglia. He and his crew suffered aircraft damage on many of those missions, but Earl was always able to bring his crew home safely in spite of the effects on their airplane by enemy opposition. They realized, as did all of the bomber and fighter airmen who flew against Germany for over 2 ½ years, that the takeoff for each mission to the Target for Today may be their last. Over 56,000 8th Air Force airmen did not return to their airbases during the course of the war. More than 26,000 were killed in action and 28,000 were Prisoners of War in German Stalags.

The columns included in this volume are not the usual tales of war stories of combat action experienced by a combat crew. Earl Wassom approaches a myriad of subjects, common experiences that each of us may have in our everyday lives, but the depth of thought and the extent of insightful evaluation and conclusions reflect the appreciation of life and lifetime values as seen through the eyes of one who has experienced the uncertainties of combat from minute to minute. His dependence on the inner strength supplied by his Maker, escalating as the war progressed, pervades this entire volume, the entire collection of *How About It!* columns.

Every ninety days I receive a column for the *8th Air Force News* from Earl. Each is eagerly read and it is always a refreshing surprise to see what is in his thoughts for the upcoming edition. In this book you will find entries that address subjects from concerts in London to death in the skies over Germany. Each is uplifting and thought-provoking, many are historical in content, but all touch the emotions of the reader.

Earl and his wife, Cynthia, are close friends of the 8th AF veterans and their spouses and both have been active in 8th Air Force organizations for a number of years. Earl has edited his 466th Bomb Group Association histories and newsmagazine, and he also served a term as President of the 2nd Air Division Association, which is comprised of fifteen bombardment groups who flew the B-24 Liberator during the war.. He presently is on the Board of Directors of the national 8th Air Force Historical Society and continues to serve as Chaplain for the organization. His Chairmanship of the NexGens initiatives of the Historical Society has attracted many of the younger generations to learn about and help preserve the legacy of the Mighty Eighth.

It is rewarding to find the *How About It!* columns edited and available in *Hello Darkee.* In this presentation, Earl worked closely with Donna Neely of Alpha Graphics Consultants. Donna has formatted each of his columns and published them in the *8th AF News* for the past decade. Readers will get an intimate look at the experiences and feelings of one who served his country in wartime and continues his love for America sixty years later.

Walter Brown, M. D.
Editor *8th AF News*
President & CEO Mighty Eighth Air Force Museum

Acknowledgements

This book would not have become a reality were it not for Dr. Walter Brown who encouraged me to begin writing "pieces" for *The Tennessee Flyover* of which he was Editor and later for the *8th Air Force Historical Society News* when he became editor of that publication. It was upon his insistence that these essays be put in book form, a project that he further supported with his suggestions, guidance and editorial skills.

To the Veterans of the Eighth Air Force who were my source of inspiration in writing these essays, I give my gratitude and appreciation.

The Mighty Eighth Air Force Museum resources have added greatly to the research endeavors of this work. Dr. Vivian Rogers Price, Research Center Director and Jean Prescott, Reference Specialist have given unselfish service in making available and permission to use the photographic files in this project.

My sincere thanks to Donna Neely and the staff of Alpha Graphic Consultants for the leadership and skills they provided. They have taken the manuscripts, photographs and graphics, and artfully arranged them for the production of this publication.

And to Cynthia my wife of sixty two years and 'my in-house editor' who has carefully read and made suggestions for the articles contained in this project.

Introduction

I consider myself to be one of the most privileged individuals in the world. Two major events occurred during my youth that shaped my outlook on life. For these, I will be eternally grateful. As a "kid" growing up in the late 1930's, food, clothing and shelter were available on a very limited basis to my family and we did not have nor did we expect any luxuries. The stock market crash affected everyone and "the Great Depression" touched every family. Unemployment was high and most Americans knew what it was to be poor. But I received moral fiber and strength during those years. The experiences of those bleak times helped formulate my outlook on life. I knew what it was like to be poor and how hard it was to earn a dollar. I learned the value of a job and compassion for those in need.

In addition to this National dilemma, hostile, greedy and ambitious political leaders in Europe and in the Orient threatened all major nations. These were subsequently drawn into a global war that engulfed Europe, Africa, Russia, China and the wide expanses of the Atlantic and Pacific Oceans. Our country and the world were in turmoil. Our President, Franklin D. Roosevelt, challenged us by saying, *"The only thing we have to fear is fear itself."* We believed him.

War is life changing. I learned this lesson from experience. At first, I was an observer but when I reached the age of 18, I became a participant. My best friend and childhood idol became a commissioned Army Air Corps pilot. He tragically lost his life in the sneak attack of Japan on Pearl Harbor, December 7, 1941. War became a reality to me. America's sudden involvement became inevitable.

A musical production by our High School students, school orchestra and teachers emphasized the theme of the war we were about to enter. The graduating Seniors in 1941 presented a play entitled *"Going My Way,"* the story of a young man leaving home and friends for duty in the military. This was a story about my friends and me. Dozens of my classmates were enlisting in the services and were on their way. Graduation exercises brought home the reality that war was bringing separations. Some of these were final and eternal.

I had always dreamed of being a flyer but the costs of flight instruction were beyond my reach. The military gave me a chance to realize my dream.

Through perseverance, diligent work, following instructions, and obedience, I was awarded my silver pilot wings and was commissioned a Second Lieutenant in the U.S. Army Air Corps. After almost a year, my initial flight training program ended and a lifetime of learning, living, and serving my country was ahead. My first assignment as an officer was to learn to fly a four-engine aircraft. Commanding a heavy bomber and training a crew of nine men was challenging. We came together as a team, ten men all with different skills and backgrounds, assigned as my crew to fly together. We soon learned each other's strengths and weakness. We learned to trust each other and we learned our assigned duties. We took seriously and we successfully completed all of the rigorous training exercises demanded of us in order to face our next assignment with confidence and courage.

We received our assignment to the 8th Air Force stationed in England and entered what many called "the Big League." There was nothing big or impressive about the Eighth in the beginning. On February 4, 1942, Ira Eaker, the newly appointed commander of this new organization, along with six staff officers left for England. They had few men, no air bases, no aircraft, no support staff. Seven months later on August 17, 1942 a modest 12 ship formation of 8th Air Force B-17 bombers flew its first mission to the marshalling yards at Rouen France. When the war ended three years later in 1945, the 8th had 350,000 men and was able to send 2,000 heavy bombers and 1,000 fighter aircraft on a single mission. During the course of this conflict, the cost was tremendous. The Eighth logged 6,537 B-17's and B-24's lost and another 3,337 fighter aircraft destroyed. Of the 210,000 combat airmen assigned to the Eighth, 56,000 were shot down. Of these, 28,000 were killed in action and another 28,000 were prisoners of war. In addition, there were another 47,000 Eighth Air Force combat airmen who were casualties Someone has said of these men who showed such courage and heroism that *"young men had to grow up or fold up; they stood strong."* They possessed a commitment to freedom and courage.

I knew a few of these men intimately during the war years. During the decades following, the association with them has become more precious. Together, we fought for freedom of the world. In the process, we developed a camaraderie known only by men who fought together and died together and some of us survived. Friends of a lifetime. ✟

Prologue

The ancient Roman city of Bath

Forty years had passed. The last time I had stood on British soil was when I went up the gangplank and boarded the former French luxury ocean liner, *Isle de France*, then being used as a troop ship. It was loaded with thousands of men. Many had completed their military assignment in the European Theatre and were being reassigned for duty elsewhere, and hundreds were battle-wounded men who were returning to the States for rest, healing, and rehabilitation.

Now, four decades later, I was back in England touring the countryside in a rented automobile. My wife and I planned a tour that gave a close-up view of the countryside that I had previously observed only from the air. We researched our trip carefully and beginning at Gatwick Airport in London, we took a clockwise circle of the country that included ten medieval and historic cities. To the south was Salisbury; then we toured the well-preserved Roman city of Bath; the seat of learning at Oxford; then, the beautiful Lake District where Shrewsbery and Chester are located; York; then the northernmost point on our trip which was Lincoln and heading back south toward Norwich in East Anglia, the area that was my war-time home.

We found a bed and breakfast in the heart of the city of Norwich. The innkeeper was most cordial. We were Americans and strangely enough, to our surprise, the Brits still loved us! He welcomed us warmly and showed us to our modest room. When he discovered that I was an airman stationed at Attlebridge, he was even more cordial and treated me as if I had won the war single-handed. He asked excitedly, "You are going to visit the Memorial Library while you are here, aren't you?" To firm up his invitation, he added, "You are within walking distance of the market place. and the Library. But you will have to wait until morning to visit it for at this late hour, it will be closed!"

Post war reunion with Wassom and co pilot Lawrence Ross (Last known survivors of Crew #554, 785th Squadron, 466th BG

My wife and I looked at each other, shrugged our shoulders and asked, "What Library? We know nothing about it."

His astonished look was followed by amazement. "You know nothing about the Library, the Memorial established here in Norfolk, to honor the 6,600 men of the Second Air Division who were killed in action in combat flights over the Continent and Germany?" "Hundreds of your veterans" he replied, "come here often to honor the memory of their fallen comrades".

When the war ended in 1945, contact with my combat comrades ended. I tried to maintain contact with my nine crewmen with whom I flew thirty-five combat missions against the Nazi War Machine. They were pleased to make contact but to continue a civilian relationship; they were disinterested. I visited those I was able to contact - one in California, one in Pennsylvania, one in New York, another in Atlanta, another in Colorado. My search ended since I was having little or no success. They were citizen soldiers and were catching up with living their lives.

This visit to Norwich opened up a new world to me. In early morning, we found the Library. It didn't open until ten and we had two hours. Even the marketplace with all of its colorful umbrellas and booths was idle. To kill time, we made our way past interesting shops along cobblestone streets to the top of the hill. The gray foreboding and dismal castle on the top of the hill looked like other ancient landmarks we had seen earlier. The centuries-old Norwich Cathedral was still awe inspiring. But, I had seen it many times before. The Library was our true goal.

Memorial Library in Norwich: l to r: Phyllis DuBois, Earl Wassom and Tony North

The Library, we learned, was the Public Library in Norwich. Inside, in a prominent first floor location, was a large room dedicated to the memory of the men of the Second Air Division, Eighth Air Force, whose lives were lost in battle. As we entered the area, we saw on the wall above shelves of books and boxes of documents, a large picture mural of B-24's in formation dropping their loads of bombs. Beneath, were replicas of the colorfully marked rudders that represented the 14 Bomb Groups of the Second Air Division. Off to the side was a small area that contained the "Roll of Honor", flags and other memorabilia. This hallowed place presented an emotional tone for the experiences that followed.

As we entered this hall, Phyllis introduced herself as the Trust Librarian and Tony as Aide to the Memorial and Library. Phyllis was an American and Tony was a true Brit who assisted her. He was an able gentleman, a historian, a writer, and very knowledgeable about the work of the Second Air Division Liberators and their crews. He was well acquainted with the 14 Second Air Division air bases that surrounded Norwich

American Military Cemetery, Cambridge, England

during the 1943-1945 war years. These two welcomed us and when we told them this was our first contact with the Library and that we knew nothing about any veterans organization, they went to the files and began bringing out documents, letters, maps and photos of my old outfit, the 466th Bomb Group; things which we did not know existed. We were given the names of contact people back in the States and an application for membership in the Second Air Division Association. They also located a volunteer to direct us to our old air base located at Attlebridge.

These volunteers of the Memorial Library told us of the American Military Cemetery located to the south of Norwich in Cambridge. "Without question, you must visit it!" they urged. Their instructions were adequate. The marker provided by the American Battle Monument Commission led us directly to the Memorial. We found it almost hidden in a tree-bordered pastoral landscape surrounded by English thatched roof houses. Old Glory was flying over the 30 acre plot of "American soil" in England where white Crosses and Stars of David mark the final resting place of 3,811 fallen airmen. Flanking the reflection pool is the Wall of the Missing with the names of an additional 5,125 who were listed as "Missing in Action." On this wall is the inscription:

Americans whose names here appear, were a part of the price that free men for the second time in a century have been forced to pay to defend human liberty and rights. All who shall live in freedom will be here reminded that to these men and their comrades we owe a debt to be paid with grateful remembrance of their sacrifice and high resolve that the cause for which they died shall live eternally. -President Dwight D. Eisenhower

Although our planned English trip was not completed, the visit to East Anglia, Norfolk, my old air base at Attlebridge, the Memorial Library in Norwich and the American Military Cemetery at Madingley had a tremendous emotional impact on me. I was anxious to get home and make contact with any veteran or organization I could. I was excited about what I had learned about veteran activities and wanted to get involved.

I filled out my application to join the 2nd Air Division Assoiciation, sent in my membership dues and within a few days, I received three back-issues of *The Journal, Official Publication of the Second Air Division Association, Eighth Air Force.* In one of those documents was an announcement, *The 50th Anniversary Celebration* commemorating the founding of the 8th Air Force. The date: January 29, 1992 and the place, Savannah, Georgia. "If we are going to get involved, now is the time." My wife agreed. We sent in our registration application and reserved a place declared to be a banquet for VIP's. I didn't feel that I fit into this

50th Anniversary Celebration of the founding of the 8th AF. First mission flow to Rouen, France August 17, 1942. Lead bombardier, Lt. Frank R. Beadle holding arming pins for the first bombs dropped by the 8th AF on the enemy

category but I sent my money and hoped for the best. I was not disappointed. I got tickets, two of the three hundred issued.

I had never been to Savannah. It was my first meeting with Veterans, comrades who were in England when I was over there. I didn't know a soul - no one knew me. But my wife and I were accepted as one of them. The lobby of the convention hotel, the Radisson, was alive with conversation coming from "old vets" wearing their frayed-cuff A-2 jackets emblazoned with the nose art of their aircraft, bombs denoting missions they had flown, and caps with the patches of their bomb group. Some wore uniforms of the yesteryears that still fit. There was a look-alike of Clark Gable. A teary eyed group were sitting before a large TV screen which documented vivid aerial combat battles and was accompanied by a rolling scroll which listed military units and the names of those lost in battle. A fighter pilot, a decorated Ace with many "kills", was autographing the book he had written. Several were gathered around a very humble-looking man, he was the recipient of the Medal of Honor.

The evening banquet for the VIP's was listed as **An Evening with the Commanders**. A receiving line was formed with thirty Generals and the wife of a deceased Commander, Mrs. Ira Eaker. I openly shed tears, as did several others, as I moved along the line shaking hands and honoring these men, our leaders, who were our war –time heroes. Dinner followed. There were 30 tables seating ten individuals; each table was graced with the presence of a General. I was a strange face among these leaders.

This was an awesome experience but I learned that men of the Eighth Air Force didn't rely alone on 50th Anniversary gatherings to get a Historical Society together. They had Conventions, Reunions, de-briefing sessions and other events just for fellowship. I met a fellow in Savannah who was President of an 8th Air Force Chapter in a neighboring state. He invited me to their next reunion. I accepted and within a few weeks I showed up at their conclave eager to get acquainted with their membership. I was not disappointed. We had much in common. We told "mission impossible stories" which got better with age, did "hangar flying" with excited voices and gesturing hands, ate and drank together, had a

Tennessee Chapter meeting: M/Gen. Lew Lyle and wife Betty, Red Harper and Earl Wassom

business meeting, conducted a memorial service remembering those no longer with us and always ended up with a banquet. Importantly, the pledge to the flag and a prayer were always part of the agenda and Eleanor, 8th AF Veteran Ned Rooks' wife, was the designated prayer.

Ned became ill and was unable to attend the next reunion. Eleanor naturally, stayed home to care for him. The Chapter was without a prayer. They cast about but there were no volunteers. Being one of the new ones in the organization, I was asked, "Can you pray?" I assured them that I did pray, probably not as effective as Eleanor, but I would give it a try. Apparently, I passed muster. As the election of officers rolled around at the next meeting, I was asked to be Chaplain.

"What about Eleanor", I asked.

"She is O.K. about it," they replied. "She has done this a long time for us and is willing to step aside and let someone else do it".

"I have never been a Chaplain. Give me a job description. What do you want me to do?

"Pray," they answered.

"Is that all? " I responded. "Well, that doesn't seem so difficult." At that moment, I became a Chaplain.

Apparently this 8th AF Chapter was looking for volunteers to carry on the work of the Society. New members were likely candidates and they preyed on them to get them involved. And new recruits, eager and excited about this new venture became willing workers. There was another neophyte who had attended the 50th Anniversary Celebration in Savannah just as I had. We did not meet there. But he too, was invited to the same Chapter Meeting that I attended. Walt Brown, being new as I, was asked to become Editor of the *The Fly Over,* the quarterly publication of the Chapter. He did a commendable job and got the editorship on a permanent basis. In fact, he performed so well that he was later given Editorship of the National Publication, *The 8th AFHS News.*

Walt, as are all Editors, was on the lookout for material to print. He came to the Chaplain and asked, "Why don't you do a column? You write something and I will print it in the *The Fly Over.*"

To sum up the scenario that followed, questions arose between the Editor and the Chaplain. What subject matter will be addressed? Shall this have a spiritual tone? How often? How long shall it be? What will we call it?

Walt the Editor: Tennessee Chapter meeting at the Ewell Farm, home of Alice and Dr. Walt Brown, with guests

The Editor gave the Chaplain free reign. Write whatever seems appropriate for the Veterans - meet their needs as you perceive them. Do about two computer pages, with double spacing. Possible titles were discussed and **"HOW ABOUT IT?** was the final choice. This title has consistently been used every time a Chaplain's article appeared. A recognizable logo unique for this "piece" was needed. The Chaplain was a pilot in the 8th Air Force. In his Bomb Group, there was an aircraft in the 784th Bomb Squadron, *Parson's Chariot,* the name given by its crew. This aircraft was not the Chaplain's, in fact, he never flew it a single time! And to clarify the matter, the Chaplain is a Chaplain in title only. He was a pilot. Our base, Station 120 at Attlebridge, had a Catholic and a Protestant Chaplain. I was not a chaplain. In fact, I was not even a man of faith when I entered the war theatre in 1944. My spiritual journey began when I uttered my first prayer, a prayer of thanksgiving when we were able to land a heavily damaged aircraft in France. The aircraft was a total loss but all ten crewmen were spared! My life had been filled with miracles but it was at this time I recognized who the Giver of miracles really was!

Since the Summer of 1993, the Editor of *The Fly Over* and *The 8th AF News* has faithfully included these articles. The Chaplain is asked often, "How do you come up with such diverse subjects?" The subject matter changes drastically from issue to issue. There is no chronological order and the events that are portrayed in these "pieces" follow no set scheme. Someone has presented the concept that *every thought that passes though our mind is conceived through creative origin.* A thought may come from reading something new, or through conversation, or personal association. A thought may come from a phone conversation, an email message, just a picture will elicit an article. A ragged-looking letter from a veteran living in a nursing home, an airman missing a limb which came as a result of exposure in a Prisoner of War camp, news of a military decoration long overdue, these events may inspire a "piece". The true emphasis of the Chaplain has been to encourage the men in their "faith walk" with God. These are the result of my desire to build and encourage the Spiritual life in all of us. A lot of time has passed since 1993 when I began writing. A lot of our men, their wives and some of their children are no longer with us. Our ranks are growing thin. One of our men said, *"I have spent entirely too much time preparing for this world and not enough for the next. I am trying to catch up."* ✝

Many of us are doing that!

Earl Wassom
466th Bomb Group, 8th Air Force
Chaplain 8th Air Force Historical Society

HELLO DARKEE

The late afternoon trip to the target was successful, so successful that Nazi night fighters were out in full force to intercept us and trail us home. As darkness fell and as visual contact among the formation worsened, enemy aircraft joined the bomber stream, blended in with the heavy bombers and followed us into the friendly skies of England. When this was recognized, immediate action was taken; all radio transmissions throughout eastern England stopped. The airwaves were silent. The principal navigational aids that were so indispensable to us, the Radio Bunchers and Splasher Beacons, were suddenly and deliberately turned off. If we used them to find our base, so could the Germans.

Below, there were no visible landmarks. All lights on the ground were extinguished. The overcast sky eliminated the possibility of celestial navigation, and all of our directional radio aids were silent. We droned on following the same heading for some time and then the navigator's message on the intercom broke the silence. "Chief", he said, "we are lost!" This was distressing news, especially from the guy who was supposed to keep track of our location at all times. An intercom conference between pilot, navigator and radio operator ensued. We recalled that the Brits had an emergency system for helping "lost and crippled" Royal Air Force planes home. We knew of it but had never used it. This was known as the "Darkee" system. Fortunately the radio frequency of this aid was in our radio operator's notes, 4,200 kilocycles.

The radio knobs were quickly turned to 4,200 kilocycles and a call went out, "Hello Darkee, Hello Darkee". We waited, then repeated our call, "Hello Darkee, Hello Darkee, this is Eglan B Baker, 'over.'" A long and drawn out silence ....then came a response, "Eglan B Baker, this is Darkee....how may I help you?" The accent was distinctively British but sounded like the voice of an angel. "Darkee, this is Eglan B Baker, we are lost...please direct us to Station 120" (this was our home base). "Roger, this is Darkee, circle and I will give you directions." In a few moments, this unseen and unpretentious subject of the King of England with a cockney accent came back on the air with a clear response, "Eglan B Baker, this is Darkee, take up a heading of 345 degrees." "Roger, Darkee, and thank you."

We settled down with our directional instructions, not knowing our exact location but feeling some assurance. In a few moments, another message from Darkee but it was not the familiar British accent we had heard before. The "different" voice gave us a directional correction, about 90 degrees to the right, an easterly heading. Before we could verify this message, again the English accent, "Hello Eglan B Baker, this is Darkee. Keep your heading of 345 degrees and follow the lights." We acknowledged but that phrase "follow the lights" was puzzling. Then, as if by magic, two vertical shafts of light from flood lamps below appeared. Then slowly they scanned downward indicating our heading and went off, then on again, vertically and sweeping downward toward our compass heading of 345 degrees. As we moved toward our base, repeatedly different shafts of light came on, directing us homeward. Another Darkee transmission informed us we were near and then suddenly, a beautiful green flare burst into the sky from almost directly below. Darkee reported, "circle to the left, you are over the field". The faint runway lights were turned on for us. We lowered our landing gear and dropped the flaps. We had safely found our home in the darkness.

Hundreds of years ago, David the King of Israel spoke these words, **"Unto the upright, there arises a light in the darkness." (Psalms 112:4 NKJ)** Back in 1944 we were guided home because we asked. We followed the simple instructions of a subject of the King. He wasn't a key military figure; he didn't get his name in headlines; he just patiently waited, silently and alone at his station with the knowledge that he and his radio transmitter were the answer to someone's survival. Today, if we ask, there is still light and truth available for all to direct us away from the enemy and to point us toward home. **"For everyone who asks receives, and he who seeks finds, and to him who knocks it will be opened." (John 7:8 NKJ)** ✝

Dum tempus habemus, operemur bonum!

Our 8th Air Force war time Commander, General "Jimmy" Doolittle in his autobiography, declares the above statement in his own unique way. He said: *"One of the privileges of age is the opportunity to sit back and ponder what you've seen and done over the years. In my nine-plus decades, I've formed some views about life and living that I have freely imposed on trusting audiences, both readers and listeners. I have concluded that we were all put on this earth for a purpose. That purpose is to make it, within our capabilities, a better place in which to live. We can do this by painting a picture, writing a poem, building a bridge, protecting the environment, combating prejudice and injustice, providing help to those in need, and in thousands of other ways. The criterion is this: If a man leaves the earth a better place than he found it, then his life has been worthwhile."*

The first quote above was penned by an individual of a different generation who was not a military man. His name was St. Francis who, near the end of his life said, *"Brothers and Sisters, while we have time, let us do good."* ✝

**Lt. General
James Doolittle**

**"One of the privileges of age
is the opportunity to sit back and ponder
what you've seen and done over the years."**

BACK TO EARTH

I raised the hand-held microphone and requested taxi instructions. The response was immediate. I released the brakes, advanced the throttles and slowly began taxing past dozens of gleaming new A-26 aircraft lined up on the hardstand, carbon-copies of the one assigned to me. At the end of the runway when my pre take-off check list was completed, I received the "green light" from the tower and started rolling. To my left was the aircraft factory which was turning out hundreds of planes for the war effort. It was over a mile long and I was airborne before I passed the end of this mountain of a building.

My Douglas A-26 Invader had less than 10 hours logged in the air. It was destined for delivery to the west coast. My assignment was to deliver it. This attack aircraft was new to the Air Force inventory. It had been in action only since November, 1944 in the 9th AF in the European Theater. I was proud to be flying it. Wherever it landed, it drew the attention of the ground "troops".

The twin 2,000 hp Pratt and Whitney eighteen cylinder engines roared majestically as I took flight. Wheels up and trimmed for climbing, the airspeed went to over 300 m.p.h. in short order. To the southwest, the sky-line of Tulsa. The mid-morning sun glistened from windows of the alabaster buildings below. The lazy Arkansas River traced a line past the tall buildings, the refineries and the rail marshalling yards. As I passed overhead, I looked down and spotted a familiar tree-lined street, a particular house which was home to a very special person.

My spirits were high. I was a native Oklahoman, and I was especially knowledgeable of the lyrics of the Broadway hit called **Oklahoma** that had put my State on the map. With the accompaniment of those two engines, I sang. Over and over, one phrase kept repeating itself in my spirit. It was, I suppose, my testimony.

> *Oh, what a beautiful morning,*
> *Oh, what a beautiful day.*
> *I've got a wonderful feeling,*
> *Everything's is going my way!*

And, everything was "going my way!" I had returned only a few weeks previously from England and the European Theater of Operations. I had successfully commanded a B-24 Liberator Bomber on thirty-five 8th Air Force combat missions into Germany along with some special assignments just as dangerous. My crew of three other officers and six enlisted men finished our "combat tour" together. I was the only one wounded, our aircraft had been damaged on several occasions and one plane was totally destroyed by enemy action. We came home together, were reassigned, went our separate ways and continued fighting the war.

Everything continued "going my way." Once back in the Zone of the Interior, my military career was reviewed and I was up for reassignment. I was given two choices. Go to B-29 transition, get experience in the "big bombers", pick up and train a new crew, and go to the Pacific Theater and fight the Japs. The other choice was the Air Transport Command, specifically the Ferry Division of the ATC. My job would be to take all kinds of airplanes any place and any time they were needed for the war effort. I made my choice on-the-spot. I would become an ATC Ferry pilot. I was reassigned immediately, was checked out in many different types of military aircraft and began my work. There were not many rules. We were permitted to choose our own routes, plan our flights and deliver aircraft to the designated location. There was one rule, however, which we had to honor. Across the United States and around the world, certain air bases were authorized refueling stops. Fortunately for me, one such authorized station was Tulsa. And, regardless of where I was in the United States, I would arrange a flight plan which led to Tulsa, and I always managed my schedule to arrive there late enough to spend the night.

Things were "going my way." Yesterday, I had spent the afternoon and evening in Tulsa at a certain address where I had written many letters while I was in England. In that house was a very attractive, desirable, "just my kind of girl." Last night, I proposed marriage. She accepted! I was engaged. Everything was going OK in Oklahoma for me. When I passed over her tree-lined street, I was tempted to give her a low-level pass and wave, but my better judgment told me that a live fiancée who was discreet in his flying practices was more valuable than a dead one.

I passed over the Red River and the familiar territory east of Dallas where I flew during my cadet flight training. I also chose San Antonio to be on my flight path. To my left was Randolph Field, the West Point of the Air. The sky was full of fledgling pilots. I flew high enough to be safe but low and close enough to give these cadets a look at a real airplane. I pushed the airspeed to the max to give them a thrill. On the west side of the city was Kelly Field alive with flight activity and a little further on, the place where aviation cadets were being mustered in and classified. There were marching formations, others were performing their PE routine, some coming, I am sure, from aircraft recognition classes. I would give them an exhibition, a fly-by of an A-26 traveling at 400 m.p.h. at an air show altitude. Did they see me? Of course! Everything was going my way. . .what a day!

Following the ATC rules to the letter, I selected an authorized ATC refueling and overnight stop in west Texas. Flying over this desolate wasteland, I continued to sing portions of the Rogers and Hammerstein hit. Along the route across Big Bend Country, I would report my position to the range stations below. It was standard operating procedure to do this and I was amazed how friendly these operators were when they responded. About twenty minutes from destination, I identified myself and called for landing instructions. They were friendly, warm, and talked me in.

There was very little air traffic and the air base at El Paso looked almost deserted. From the air it was obvious where the control tower, the flight line and base operations were located. But, when I reached the end of the runway, sitting there waiting was the Jeep to direct me in. But three men

Wassom emerging from the cock-pit of an A-26, the view the disgusted "greeting committee" saw when they were expecting a glamorous female pilot

manned it, not the customary one GI. Mounted across the rear of the Jeep was the usual yellow and black striped sign declaring FOLLOW ME. Kneeling down and peering over the sign and looking back were two of the three occupants, smiling and waving enthusiastically. "Friendly Texas GI's," I mused. I obediently followed the yellow Jeep. As we approached the flight line, I noticed a number of military ground vehicles of all types surrounded by two or three dozen GI's. They were all happy, waving, grinning from ear-to-ear. "What is this all about?" I asked myself again.

The three blades of the Hamilton Standard Props came to a halt, I did the usual procedures to shut down the engines, the radio, and fill out my flight report. The GI's just stood there waiting. I opened the canopy, unfastened my seat belt, reached for my belongings and elevated myself from the bucket seat and extracted my 200 pound 6'3" frame from the A-26. The waiting crowd looked on with astonishment and loudly uttered some explicatives, indignantly got in their vehicles and left the scene in a cloud of dust and smoke. Not one remained! I was alone on the flight line. I flung my seat type parachute over my shoulder, picked up my B-4 bag and walked three or four hundred yards in the Texas July heat to the Operations Building wondering what had gone wrong with my "wonderful day."

The cigar chomping First Lieutenant standing behind the counter peered at me and said in no uncertain terms "You have damn near ruined the morale of this entire base." I suddenly had a sinking feeling that my "wonderful day" was just about down the tube! He did, however, offer an explanation. "We have had reports of your coming clear across Big Bend Country. Even I anticipated your arrival. Your high pitched voice on the radio convinced everyone along the way that a WASP (Women's Air Force Service Pilot) was ferrying a plane to El Paso. We, in this God-forsaken place, have seen very few of these beautiful female pilots pass through here."

"So that was it!" I finished checking in, made my way to the BOQ, found the mess hall, ate and planned my next move. Should I place a telephone call in to Tulsa, call my fiancée of 20 hours standing? Or would she wonder who the sultry-sounding female calling long-distance could be? If I placed the call, would this tragically end a wonderful day where everything was going my way? "Well, it is worth the risk," I mused. And it was!

We just celebrated our 60th wedding anniversary and my voice still registers in the upper range! Tenor anyone? ☦

The glamorous female WASP they were expecting

WHY FEAR?

World War I, the war that was supposed to "end all wars," left the world more fearful than before. Chaos and unrest were still present. The war solved few problems and created more. The struggle among nations caused more fear and there was little leadership with integrity. Men with greed and controlling spirits arose as political firebrands. Their sole purpose was to conquer. The tired, fearful and hungry people turned to the available leadership. In China there was Mao, Franco pronounced himself as leader in Spain, Lenin controlled Russia, Benito Mussolina saw himself as a savior who would rescue his country from chaos. Adolf Hitler transformed Germany into a militant camp. These radical leaders slowly gathered support and formed partnerships for disaster.

As the world became increasingly infected with conflict, the United States attempted to stay neutral but war knows no bounds. Soon there was Pearl Harbor and the aggressive military moves of Japan thrust America into war. Soon after, the U.S. declared war on Germany. With losses in the Pacific,

Adolph Hitler, arrogant leader of the Nazi Movement whose boastful pride proclaimed himself to be the future leader of the world. "Heil Hitler"

Africa, Europe, there was no good news anywhere. People were becoming demoralized and fearful. The President of the United States in one of his radio addresses said, *"We have nothing to fear but fear itself."* This challenge to the people of the nation was very timely. Fear is a deadly thing; it is contagious and can spread like a plague.

None of us are immune to fear. It touches everyone and must be dealt with individually. How to do this? In the Chinese language, the word for ***crisis*** is a combination of two other words, **danger** and **opportunity.** The crises of life create danger with the response being fear. Fear must be acknowledged and then determination made as to what opportunities are available to overcome it.

Air crew members faced a crisis every time a combat mission was flown. I have to yet find an individual who did not experience fear. He might try to ignore it, but it existed. A squadron commander, who outranked most of the men on base and who had more flying and combat experience than they, confessed long after the war his true feeling regarding fear. All alone at night in his hut, he would hear an aircraft engine in the distance sputter to life, then increase to a mighty roar, then die out. The maintenance crew was making last minute adjustments, tuning the engine. Fear gripped him as he thought of the next day's mission, his responsibilities for the men of his squadron and for himself. He also recognized that fear is an insidious and deadly thing which can warp judgment and reduce effectiveness. He thought of all of the dangers he would face, he reviewed in his mind all of the emergency procedures and felt security, but that alone did not assure him of a safe return. He might die.

His father, a veteran himself, shared earlier with his son a comforting scripture and he read once again, the 91st Psalm. *"His faithful promises are your armor and protection. Do not be afraid of the terrors of the night nor fear the dangers of the day, nor dread the plague that stalks in darkness, nor the disaster that strikes at midday. . . If you make the Lord your refuge, if you make the most High your shelter, no evil will conquer you. . . I will rescue those who love me. I will protect those who trust in my name. When they call me, I will answer, I will be with them in trouble. I will rescue them and honor them. I will satisfy them with a long life and give them my salvation." (Psalms 91 NLT)*

This commander knew very well what might happen on the upcoming mission. He knew fear would ride with him but he could live with it. In its proper place, fear would be an asset, sharpening his skills, keeping him alert and effective. He did all he knew to do, he handed it over to God, and no matter what happened, he knew God would be with him, in this world or the next!

As human beings, on our last mission, we face certain death. It will come to all of us. The certainties of death can be met with confidence. God will be with us in this world and the next as well. God declares, "Fear not" and with faith in Him, we need not fear. ✝

WHY WAIT?

Regardless of age or station in life, everyone has his mind focused on something that is going to come up in the future. Baby's birth, his first tooth, first step, first haircut, are events remembered by the proud parents.

A G.I. enjoying a small pleasure

Children anticipate their birthday, first day of school, a true friend and playmate. Adolescents look forward to owning their own automobile, first date, independence from authority, graduation and life. Those entering into adulthood consider falling in love, careers, college, marriage, starting a home and a family. Older folks look at life that seems to be going by too fast and anticipate problems such as health, finance, and the welfare of their grown children and grandchildren.

Looking to the future and planning for it is a normal and healthy pursuit. But, things once anticipated soon become a part of our memory and are history. As we reflect on some experiences, we feel pleasure and rejoice in them. Other things we remember and review them with regret, such as the bad choices we have made. Our visions for the future may be wonderful dreams, which will be realized many times. Sometimes, our choices turn out to be bad dreams. And so, life is made up of looking back or looking forward, with either joy or remorse. We are grateful for the past and look forward to the future. But someone has said, "The past is like a cancelled check, the future is a promissory note, what about today?"

Right now, you are in possession of this moment. You can control it. Yesterday's moment is vanished. Tomorrow's moment is uncertain. A very perceptive songwriter captured the essence of this idea. *"We have this moment to hold in our hands and to clutch, as it sifts through our fingers like sand. Yesterday is gone and tomorrow may never come. We have this moment today." (Gaither).*

Edgeworth wrote: *"There is no moment like the present. The man who will not execute his resolutions when they are fresh upon him can have no hope from them afterwards."* To put this exercise into practice, take a deep breath and think of three things for which you are grateful, right at this moment. A happy person is not a person in a certain set of circumstances, but rather a person with a certain set of attitudes. Some attitudes to consider are:

- **Put others first.**
- **Have fun and enjoy small pleasures.**
- **Give all you have today.**
- **Take care of what you can and leave the rest to God.**

Lord, help me to be aware that today will never return. Give me a sense of stewardship for the life you grant me, that will make me want this day to count for good. Amen. ✝

IN PERSPECTIVE

There is a trite saying, which has been around a long time. Many folks live their life and make important decisions based on this rather weak philosophy. Some actually believe the "grass is greener on the other side." Cattle are not among the most intelligent creatures of God's creation but many folks copy their behavior and act very similar to livestock. We have observed cows standing knee-deep in lush green grass eyeing the field on the "other side of the fence." Invariably, they inch toward the obstacle that stands between them and the prize on the other side. They turn and twist their necks, navigating their head between the sharp barbed wires in an effort to nuzzle their heads to the grass that looks more inviting than that where they are standing. In the process of executing this maneuver, they cannot avoid the peril of the sharp prongs on the fence and come out the loser and although bloody and torn, are still convinced that the "other side" is better.

Some folks want a "quick fix" for a temporary trial or problem that has arisen in their lives. They look to others who seemingly have made a change to remedy their unhappiness or dilemma. They see the external changes that have occurred with others but haven't observed the total cost in the final and hidden outcomes of the changes they have made. Sudden apparent prosperity and success of someone else may lure the uninformed to give up true and tried security to try the "grass" on the other side. Upon closer observation, there may be cuts and bruises that might make such a new venture unwise. Perhaps a marriage has become uninteresting and a new mate seems to be the answer. Be careful! Years of nurturing, sharing, loving, laughing, weeping, happiness and sorrow can be lost in a few unwise moments in actions and thoughts spent looking around. The list could go on and on. There are appropriate times when change can advisably be made. But these should be made only after serious prayer and thought is given to the "grass" on your side of the fence.

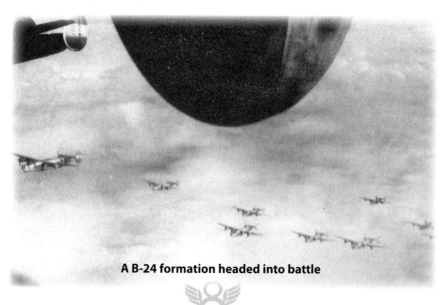

A B-24 formation headed into battle

A man wrote a letter to his friends. He was a good citizen of his country and through a series of trials and mistrials, he was judged guilty and was placed in prison. In fact, he was on death row awaiting his execution. He encouraged his friends to be united in prayer, and be joyful. Paul the Apostle had everything in perspective when he penned his letter. He wrote: . . .*"I have learned in whatever state I am, to be content". (Colossians 4:11 NKJ)*

Just recently I had conversation with a WW II infantryman. He told me of his participation in the D-Day invasion, his trek with the ground forces across France under General George Patton's leadership and ultimately the confrontation of American and British forces with the Germans in what we have called the Battle of the Bulge. I listened to his story and remarked to him: "Whenever I flew over the battle front and looked down and saw you guys engaged in hand-to-hand fighting and the terrible conditions under which you were living, I felt real admiration, but I was certainly glad I was not down there with you." He replied: "So, you were up there in those four-engine bombers with two big tails! What a beautiful sight seeing all of those hundreds of friendly aircraft flying in support of us. But, seeing Americans flying up there and the Germans shooting away at you, we felt that you didn't have a chance if you took a hit from those German 88mm guns blasting away at you. I was glad I was down on solid earth."

There you have it. Both of us liked the "grass" on our side of the fence. We must learn the secret of being content where we are. What is green to some may not be that appealing to you. Let us strive to live at peace with yourself, with God, and to live contented in every situation where life has placed you! *"...be content with such things as you have. For He Himself has said, 'I will never leave you nor forsake you.' "* *(Hebrews 13:5 NKJ)*

✞

The enemy responds. Flak at nine o'clock!

25

AMERICA, BLESS GOD

In times of crisis, America turns its heart to God and Country. The flag is flown and displayed with pride. The National Anthem is sung with greater emotion, meaning and gusto. Patriotic songs recognizing and honoring God become popular once again. The theme. *"God bless America, land that I love, stand beside her and guide her, through the night with the light from above"* is embraced with humility and verified with watery eyes.

We have every reason to be appreciative for what our Creator has done for us as individuals and as a country. What started over two hundred years ago as a new experiment in forming a government *"of the people, by the people and for the people"* has been a great success. The development of this new concept of self-rule has, across the years, faced many obstacles and challenges from within and certainly by envious outsiders who long for the freedom the citizens of this country enjoy. Across the years, peoples of other countries have sought refuge in America. With unrest on the increase throughout the world, the flow of immigrants is swelling. And why shouldn't they seek refuge here?

God has *"blessed America."* Check out your own ancestry. What skills and educational backgrounds did they bring with them to America? Yet, with all of the religious, ethnic, racial and social diversity of Americans throughout the United States, we have blended into a homogenous population with one purpose and goal, to preserve those individual rights for which our nation was formed. We started out as a government with a few colonies that came to grips with the idea of independence and self-governance. That concept has expanded to include all fifty of our states. Our citizens have freedom to choose their vocations, where they live, their social group, how they worship, how they vote, where they go, their life-style, all of which comes with no interference from the government. From this, Americans have developed a "caring" spirit, not only for ourselves but for the people of the world, our charitable giving is unequalled.

God has blessed America, and the rest of the world through America as well, because of her spirit of generosity. Our Allies would not have survived WWII without America's involvement in that war. Following the peace, America poured in billions of dollars and forgave other billions of dollars in debts to our Allies and enemies alike. None of these countries even today are paying the interest on these debts to the United States. Whenever earthquakes hit distant continents, it is the United States who hurries in with help. When disasters of floods, tornadoes, hurricanes or earthquakes come to our shores, very few help us. The generosity of America in sending our military forces to bring stability to weak nations where the citizens are oppressed, or sending billions of dollars as aid to quell starvation, has often been meet with the chant "warmongers." The countries of the world choose our Jumbo jets in great quantity for their airlines. Our superior military hardware is in much demand everywhere. Our technology advances exceed the developments of any country in the world. Why? American ingenuity produces what other countries cannot. Hundreds of times, Americans have raced to help other people in trouble. This help comes not only from the government but also through the "hearts" of people who give through charitable organizations to provide food, medical supplies, shelter and hope. This is the character of the United States of America!

God Bless America. He has. He does. He will continue to do so. He has also blessed the world and will continue to do so as long as we honor Him. This brings me to the subject of this article. It is time for America to bless God. How do we bless God? Through honor and worship. Two thousand years ago, Paul the Apostle described the attitude necessary to honor and worship God. He said, *"We bless those who curse us. We are patient with those who abuse us. We respond gently when evil things are said about us"* (I Corinthians 4:12-13 NLT) Doesn't this sound like the spirit of America? The writer of the Book of Proverbs broadened this concept when he declared. *"Godliness exalts a nation, but sin is a disgrace to any people." (Proverbs 14:34 NLT)* We as a nation and as individuals have received everything from the Almighty. Now is the time for AMERICA to BLESS GOD! ✝

Veterans gathering at a reunion to remember their comrades who paid the supreme sacrifice and to give thanks

CHECK YOUR GOALS

Remember the story, *Alice in Wonderland*? At one point in the story, Alice stops at the crossroads. Sitting there was a Cheshire Cat. Alice approached him and asked which road to take. The Cat responds by asking where she wants ago. She tells him that it "doesn't much matter where." "Then it doesn't matter which way you go," he replies. As a result, she wanders aimlessly in her travels.

Our first response could be, "Well, she was young and inexperienced." Or, "She was uncertain and didn't really know where to go." But, there are individuals in all age categories whose examples indicate that it is not youth or uncertainty which create this dilemma in making life changing decisions. Like Alice, we often travel the road of life without specific goals or direction. Someone said, *"If you don't know where you are going, how will you know when you get there?"*

What is a goal? In the arena of sports, it is an area or object toward which players in various games attempt to advance a ball or puck. The same concept applies to human endeavor outside of sports; that is, a willful effort or an assignment undertaken by an individual to aim for a dream or ambition of life and achieve it. What is your goal? Select anything, anything of your choosing, then go for it! Who are goals for? Anyone, at any age.

"Where there is no vision (goal), the people perish" (Proverbs 29:18 KJV)

Often times, however, we have a wrong concept of what a goal really is. Usually, we're looking for the big things which impress the public and which will inflate our egos. We are prone to seek out the big calling, the big challenge. It was Bonhoeffer who expressed the thought *"We think we dare not be satisfied with the small measure of spiritual knowledge, experience and love that has been given to us, and that we must constantly be looking forward eagerly for the highest good."* He developed this idea by saying: *"Be grateful even where there's no great experience and no discoverable riches, but much weakness, small faith, and difficulty."*

An individual wearing the military uniform of his country is aware of the fact that one day, he will encounter the enemy and will face the reality that death may occur. He has as a goal, survival and a safe return to his loved ones back home. There is nothing wrong with this, but there may be more important goals which he will achieve as he pursues his primary goal of survival. A paratrooper named Al assigned to the 101st Airborne Division parachuted into Normandy on D-Day, June 6, 1944. On D Day plus three, he was hit by enemy fire. Joe, his good friend, a platoon sergeant, had the identical goal of survival as Al. But a greater goal presented itself in combat as he saw his injured friend on the battlefield. He risked his life to drag him to cover and safety. This was a short-term goal of opportunity. Al survived to return to battle after seven weeks of hospitalization. This "window of opportunity" came quickly, the response was rapid, the results were positive and both Al and Joe were recipients of an achieved goal of opportunity.

Our BIG goals are interspersed with short-term goals of opportunity. They may not make a huge splash in the eyes of observers but a kind word, a letter of appreciation, a prayer of consolation, a smile or pat on the back are always welcome.

If we are content with who we are, there are all kinds of opportunities. Will we reach for them? Life will be "sweeter" if we do! ☩

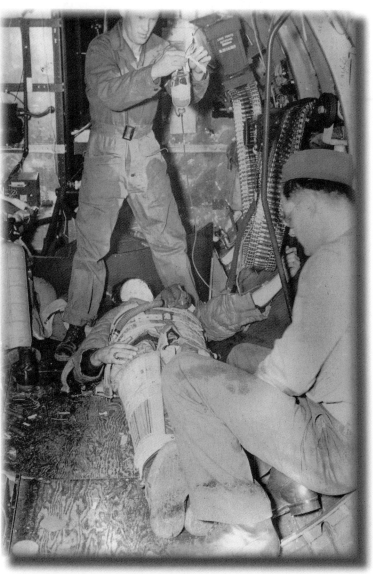

An airman administering first aid to a wounded buddy

HOLD ON

Ten years ago in Savannah, Georgia, " happy warriors" of the Mighty Eighth Air Force gathered for the 50th anniversary celebration of the founding of the 8th Air Force. Men and women who had served in almost every duty assignment on airbases throughout East Anglia, both aircrew members and ground support staff, were present. There was no "uniform of the day." Suits, casual wear, informal garb, but noticeable among the crowd of participants were men wearing original A-2 G.I. issue jackets. These carried bits of unrecorded history with them. They were old, frayed, faded, but the messages of the yesteryears still spoke loudly. Aircraft names were given, appropriate artwork representing girl friends or wives back home or fictitious dream girls were portrayed in gorgeous form. The number of missions flown and the number of enemy aircraft kills were displayed with painted bombs or swastikas on the worn frayed jackets. Notable destinations such as Regensburg, Schweinfurt, Berlin, Ploesti, Kassel, Hamburg and others were listed with pride as the battlefields in the skies, the places where they fought and friends died.

Martin J. Ryan, Jr. Lt./Gen in a letter dated 23 January 1992 wrote: *"I am honored to command the Eighth Air Force as it approaches its 50th Anniversary. Today's descendents of the proud World War II organization is still mighty and recently returned to its roots as the exclusive domain of the nation's long-range bomber force."* He further stated: *"I count it a privilege to designate 28 January through 1 February 1992 as the anniversary of the 'Mighty Eighth.' Let airmen everywhere pause to remember the world's greatest air armada and dedicate themselves to the second 50 years of guarding freedom and keeping the peace."*

Another decade has rolled by and it is now 2002. We are in the 60th Anniversary Year of the Mighty Eighth. During the past ten years, the Eighth Air Force has guarded the skies of the free world, has encountered and defeated the enemy, has insured peace and is even now engaged! Many men of courage, from Commanders to followers have folded their wings since 1992. They are no longer with us. We honor their memory and at the same time acknowledge our Creator who sustained life to those of us who remain. We must not consider ourselves anything less than blessed with life itself! Look around to those of us who remain. We are not big or little, important or unimportant, we are all equal!

At the 50th Anniversary Celebration

Oswald Chambers wrote:

"…We never dream that all the time God is in the commonplace things and people around us."

Dietich Bonhoeffer also talked about small things saying: *"We prevent God from giving us the great spiritual gifts He has in store for us, because we do not give thanks for daily gifts…Only he who gives thanks for little things receives the big things."*

In the foyer of the convention hotel at the 50th, a TV was running continuously showing footage of the 8th AF in action. A second tape rolled, a tribute to comrades less fortunate than the viewers. The seemingly endless lists of squadrons and the deceased airmen in those units were listed. The viewers watched with moist eyes as they listened to the background music that filled the foyer of the hotel. The words of the old but familiar church hymn correctly portrayed the true emotions of those watching.

> *Through many dangers, toils and snares,*
> *I have already come.*
> *His grace has brought me safe thus far,*
> *And grace will lead me home.*

When the colors were presented, a twenty-one gun salute was offered, and "Taps." was played, the participants of this 50th reunion did not glory in their successes in civilian life or their military careers, but realized with gratitude once again that they were walking, living miracles; all of them! Now, ten years later, grace is still leading us home. We have held on. We will continue to "hold on" to those things dearest to us. Hold on to our God, our faith and one another. God is with us, even in the smallest details of our lives! ✞

Fifty years later, Veterans gathering at the Bull Street Armory, Savannah, Georgia, to remember and celebrate the beginning of the 8th AF.

CHECK POINTS

Hundreds of B-17 and B-24 Eighth Air Force bombers were flying formation high in the frigid air heading westward. The heavies were returning from a combat mission deep in enemy territory. Some were flying without difficulty. Others, damaged by enemy action, were struggling to stay in the air. They had been in a hostile environment for over seven hours facing fighters, flak, and mechanical problems. They were homeward bound. Up ahead and to the west, as far as the eye could see, was a solid bank of clouds which blocked the sight of the cold waters of the North Sea below. The sight of land and the airbase that these airmen called home was also blocked from their view. This covering of clouds, rain and fog reaching almost to the ground was the last obstacle they had to face on this mission. It had to be safely penetrated before the mission was completed.

The Modern Chapel of the Fallen Eagles in Savannah, Georgia

The twelve ship squadrons were flying in tight formation. Over enemy territory a close-knit pattern of aircraft was the hallmark of a well trained, disciplined and effective air combat unit. It ensured a concentration of combined firepower of each ship's ten guns against enemy fighter aircraft attacking the formations and also ensured a tight pattern of bombs falling on the target. But now, with poor visibility down below, instrument flying would be required. Formation flying, under these weather conditions, is impossible. Until now, the responsibility of the large formation of aircraft rested upon the Commander. At this point, each pilot had to assume responsibility for the fate of his aircraft and the nine other members of his crew.

The procedures were well established for this instrument let-down. It was dependent upon each pilot to execute the plan precisely. When the squadron was in its properly designated position, each individual aircraft executed a turn around back to the designated radio beacon and began its descent. Each aircraft followed at thirty-second intervals.

The rate of descent was established, the murky mass of clouds began rushing silently beneath. Thirty seconds ahead, the lead aircraft slowly disappeared into the undercast. In moments, we would be there ourselves, alone and on our own! Suddenly, the aircraft was engulfed in the gray mass as it followed behind the path of our leader. Moisture formed on the windows fogging visibility even further. Thirty seconds behind was another aircraft and another and still another following one by one until all of the planes and crews in the Group were in the stream. There was no room for error.

The Medieval Norwich Cathedral

Ahead, there was no visible horizon, only blackness and rain. The instruments on the panel before the pilot and the din of a radio signal were his only sources of orientation. The watchful eyes of the co pilot, flight engineer, and navigator on the flight deck added moral support to the pilot, but they could do little to help him but watch. As the altimeter wound down and as the ground grew closer, there was still no visual contact. A welcome navigation light flashing on the instrument panel indicted we were on course. This beacon was the signal to make the turn toward our 150 foot wide and 6,000 foot long runway. Slowly, the heavy clouds turned into mist and fog. The trees, hedgerows, thatched-roof houses were dimly visible through the murk. On our left and through the haze, the 315 foot tall spire of the Norwich

Cathedral stood in all of its majesty. That 15th century steeple had guided people to God for 500 years and was a welcome check point now leading us home. Reassuringly, another light on the panel flickered; we were moments away from our runway. To the right, the quaint moss-covered medieval All Saints Church came into view, a second check point. This landmark was just off the end of the runway we were seeking. Worshippers from the villages, past and present, found spiritual comfort in this little church and the message it proclaimed. The tires on the plane screeched as we touched the runway. Another mission was completed. Faith in our airplane, the confidence we had in our training and our comrades, the timely check points and the awesome God who was worshipped in the Norwich Cathedral and the All Saints Church brought us safely to our home base again.

It is often impossible to revisit these timeless check-points in East Anglia, England. But, while driving down Interstate I-95 through the muggy atmosphere near Savannah, the sight of a rising stone bell tower replicating the medieval All Saints Church in East Anglia will perhaps cause people to think of God and thank Him for His sacrifice and the sacrifices of the intrepid warriors of the Eighth Air Force in 1942-1945. The message of **The Chapel of the Fallen Eagles** is welcoming all of us home. Located in the Memorial Gardens of the Mighty Eighth Air Force Museum, the Chapel is a memorial to those who paid the supreme sacrifice as well as those who survived. It serves as a constant reminder to us to worship and praise our Savior who has so wonderfully given us life in Him. . . salvation, redemption, peace, happiness and the promise of a safe landing for eternity. ✞

UNBENDING BUT FLEXIBLE

At a recent military reunion, one veteran stood up and announced to the group that the average age of the membership was 79. Another spoke up: "I don't know why you have to broadcast it; one look at you doesn't require an announcement." There is a simple explanation for the continuous longevity of veterans of the Eighth Air Force. They just keep hanging around until they reach the 100 year mark and then are very careful. The goal of one guy on his 100th birthday was to live until he was 125 and then die from a gunshot wound inflicted by a jealous husband.

Not many folks reach the century mark. But isn't it amazing how many good things just keep happening to our generation? Count up the number of decades that we have survived. The many events in our lives, some enjoyed and others endured, are amazing! Life began in the 1920's for many of us. The 1930's call up many wonderful events that bring smiles to our faces and many happy memories. The 1940's were full of many, many momentous experiences - a global war, educational opportunities, marriage, a career, a family, and without doubt, our first home mortgage. Add more ten-year periods and the old century has quickly passed and a new one begun. The twenty-first century has presented new faces in Washington, D.C.; new personalities, both good and bad, on the TV screens; economic swings; and sadly, new wars and violence all over the world. These periods on the calendar do nothing but measure time. Time, is the moment where we are living right now.

We are now consumed by a technological revolution. We fliers of WWII had as our mentors, commanders who were the true pioneers of flight and the dreamers and planners deciding the direction aviation would go. Pilots and crewmen who trained under them were given the challenges of their pioneering spirit. Then we flew "by the seat of our pants." Now modern pilots "fly by wire". Then we flew aircraft that were "state of the art", the largest, fastest most rugged our country could provide at that time. But the war brought modifications to the aircraft and the needed changes in the techniques required to better utilize our equipment. Our leaders and combat experiences were constantly demanding modification. Change was required. If we didn't change, it was "goodbye world." A street-corner philosopher stated; "Even if you are on the right track, you can get run over if you just sit there."

Our generation produced the "baby boomers" and they, in turn, procreated the next crop of children who have been dubbed "Generation X". Our age should not be allowed to limit us. Our grandchildren are constantly challenging our generation to keep up. Things common-place now were not even invented during our days of growing up. Computers, FAX machines, cell phones, television, VCR's, medical diagnostic techniques, pagers, e-mail, satellites, and the internet network have broadened our world of learning and thinking and the way things are done. We should remain current and keep in touch with the present generation. Technology changes the environment in which we live but does not change who we are. We must be flexible but at the same time be unbending in maintaining and up-holding the moral and spiritual values which were such a vital ingredient of our generation. We are products of our spiritual roots and we must keep them and pass them on.

When we reach the end of our days, a moment or two from now, we should be able to look backward to something more meaningful than the pursuit and achievement of wealth or the utilization of technology. Our earthly existence will have been wasted unless we have experienced and given love, made a worthwhile investment in the lives of others and earnestly attempted to serve the God who made us and who gives to each of us new life and hope every day.

"I will put my spirit in you and you shall live." (Ezekiel 37:14 NKJ) ✝

How About It?

War machines have changed, man's basic needs never change

SHOWDOWN EVERYDAY

Sir Arthur Harris, Air Chief Marshall of the RAF Bomber Command, received orders to build a bomber force to strike at the heart of Nazi Germany. He inherited a very small contingent of dedicated aircrew men, a small assortment of obsolescent aircraft, and orders that were not clearly defined. From these meager beginnings, he built a Command, which at the beginning of the war was only able to mount token raids on German targets. At the close of the war and his tenure as Marshall of Bomber Command, he could dispatch 1,000 planes on a nightly basis. There was a tremendous price paid for these successes. There were 55,564 RAF men killed in combat over the skies of Germany during this time, a loss rate of 51 per cent of the 110,000 Bomber Command aircrew members assigned to him.

His personal sacrifice was tremendous as well. He had 18 hour days and worked tirelessly for three years with seldom a day of leave. He was exhausted. In his 1947 memoirs, **Bomber Offensive,** he wrote:

> *I wonder if the frightful mental strain of commanding a large air force in war can ever be realized except by those who have experienced it. While a Naval commander may at the most be required to conduct a major action once or twice in the whole course of a war, and an Army commander fights a battle say once in six months or, in exceptional circumstances, once a month, the commander of a bomber force has to commit the whole of it every twenty-four hours.*

Not only did military commanders face an occasional military showdown, air crew members encountered life or death situations every day. Thinking of facing combat again and again was always an emotional experience. Fear never went away. As long as there were missions to fly, the pressure was on.

And so it is, not only in war, but also in daily living throughout life. From birth to death there is a daily pressure. Our total perspective on the quality of our life style depends upon our attitude and approach to life. We all face a daily show down with everyday events. We have "good" days and other days that are not so good. In observing two individuals, each of whom have similar opportunities and equal circumstances, one lives a very fulfilled life, the other an empty existence. Why the difference? Psychologists used to believe that if a person is properly *stimulated*, then a proper *response* will follow. But, real life situations indicate that stimulation alone does not always produce the desired behavior. There is another element, the *organism*, or the will of the individual himself that determines the results.

Admirals, Generals and Air Commanders have their occasional opportunities for military victories and/or defeats during their careers. But every individual faces challenges over which they can win every day of their life. Struggles? Certainly! Paul the Apostle expressed his belief that we can be winners when he gave a number of circumstances we all face in daily living. He declared that a daily walk with God will make all of our encounters with life more victorious when he said:

"…nothing can separate us from the love of God …Death can't and life can't. The angels can't, and the demons can't. Our fears for today, our worries about tomorrow, and even the powers of hell can't keep God's love away. Whether we are high above the sky or in the deepest ocean, nothing in all creation will ever be able to separate us from the love of God that is revealed in Christ Jesus our Lord." (Romans 8:38-39 NLT)

God has a plan for each of us. God nudges us along but He never over-rules our will. He has a plan as to whom we can be. Our close and on-going relationship with God will reveal what He wants and expects of us and it is up to us to follow. ✝

Another night mission for Royal Air Force Airmen

NO SUBSTITUTE

Vince Lombardi, the icon of American football competition, was the legendary coach of the Green Bay Packers. This team, under his leadership, won (between 1960 to 1968) five NFL championships, including three consecutive trophies and the first two Super Bowl games. Lombardi believed and taught his players that there was no substitute for victory.

This concept was ingrained in the citizens of the United States from its beginnings. Although America's citizenship was made up of people of all classes and nationalities, they had a winning spirit. The earliest pilgrims, the founding fathers, the settlers of the Great West were winners. They were dauntless. Defeat was not in their vocabulary. God, family, country and neighbors were important. Their freedom was priceless and when it was challenged, they were always ready to defend it. Theoretically they and their government preferred   peace and sought to avoid conflict but when war seemed inevitable, they determined "there was no substitute for victory."

Pearl Harbor, December 7, 1941

In the late 1930's, Europe was on the verge of conflict, but the U.S. viewed it as "their war". They felt that there was time to decide what our involvement should be. Then, all of a sudden, Germany's militant moves that conquered Poland and the Lowlands stunned Washington. When France surrendered to

German forces shortly thereafter, the evacuation of the British Expeditionary Force at Dunkirk left Europe totally in the hands of the Nazis. There was only the English Channel and the resolve of the Brits to determine the outcome, victory or defeat. There were rumors that Germany's super race had secret new weapons of mass destruction, super-submarines, long-range bombers, and other super-weapons. Washington was hesitant to make any commitment until December 7, 1941 when the Japanese attacked Pearl Harbor. America was shocked into reality A world war was inevitable and the American citizens rallied to the cause when President Roosevelt spoke of "the dastardly sneak attack on Pearl Harbor by the Empire of Japan". Immediately following, war was declared on Japan and Germany, the Axis Powers.

As it stood, Italy could soon control the Mediterranean, Hitler could take charge of Europe and the former British and French empires, Japan could dominate the Pacific area and China. America felt secure with oceans all about her, but her isolationism and indifference for decades had left her weak. In fact, America's military was able to field fewer than 300,000 soldiers at that time. Airpower was almost nonexistent, and the Navy suffered great losses in the early 1942's.

The prevailing attitude can be summed up in the following hypothetical story about four people: *Everybody, Somebody, Anybody, and Nobody.* There was an aggressor which had to be eliminated and *Everybody* in America was sure that *Somebody* would do it. *Anybody* could have done it, but *Nobody* did. *Somebody* got angry about it because it was *Everybody's* job. *Everybody* thought *Anybody* could do it, but *Nobody* realized that *Everybody* wouldn't do it. It ended up that *Everybody* blamed *Somebody* when actually *Nobody* asked *Anybody*. But, when challenged by the President, the USA became what he described as the *Arsenal of Democracy.* Within three years,

41

How About It?

industry, labor, military leadership, politicians, men, women, children began a mighty crusade to achieve victory. Resources were taken from the earth, were diverted to factories everywhere, crafted by workmen into weapons, transferred to theatres of war and used by newly trained warriors to achieve the victory. *Everybody* pitched in. *Everyone* agreed that there was no substitute for victory. Great victories are the result of a passion. Passion is the result of dedication to a cause greater than our selfishness. ✞

IN PERSPECTIVE

Every generation wants to be helpful. In order to stimulate the thinking of my nine year-old grandson about his future studies, I took him to the campus where I spent my final years as a professor in academe. I pointed out the dormitories where the students lived when away from home while they were in college. He responded, "Grandpa, what kind of bird is that?" Undaunted, I showed him the huge arena explaining that this university was very proud of its basketball team. The building was named to honor the coach who was one of the most winning coaches in the history of basketball and in that big round building, over twelve thousands fans would gather cheering for their team. "Grandpa, look at those trees. Aren't they big?" I pointed out the newly dedicated one hundred forty-five foot bell tower We waited until the chimes struck on the hour. As the sounds echoed across the beautiful campus, I explained that this tower was built to honor a brave student who, as a soldier, had given his life for his country. I saw a sparkle in his eyes, but he was not looking upward, but downward. He responded, "Grandpa, look at this strange-looking insect. Isn't it beautiful?" This 79 year-old grandfather decided things are different when seen through the eyes of a 9 year-old.

Age is not the only area where differences are noticeable. A fine country fellow got himself a date with a beautiful city girl. On a secluded hill above the little village, they sat enthralled at the nocturnal events surrounding them. He loved the night sounds of the country and especially the sounds of the crickets doing their nightly serenades. The girl was also enchanted in this environment. From below, a band was playing a concert in the park. Classical music filled the girl's ears. She said, "Aren't the sounds we are hearing beautiful? " His face was beaming as he looked at her and he answered, " Yes, and I understand they do it by rubbing their back legs together!"

In perspective, outlook on life varies with age and with cultural differences. However, regardless of these characteristics, there is a common ground if we can honestly answer this question. *Upon what are we building our life?* Our life is limited if it is self-centered and self-serving. Our life must be built on the true foundation of the Lord. I read these words from the notes of an American Legion Chaplain. *"Your task,"* God said, *" is to build a better world."* I answered, *"How? The world is so large and complicated and I am so small and useless; there is nothing I can do."* But God in all His wisdom said, *"Just build a better you!"*

And how do we do this?
"Then said Jesus unto his disciples, 'If any man will come after me, let him deny himself, and take up his cross, and follow me. For whosoever will save his life shall lose it: and whosoever will have lost his life for my sake shall find it For what is a man profited if he shall gain the whole world and lose his own soul? Or what shall a man give in exchange for his soul?'" (Matt.16:24-26 KJV)

Your age doesn't matter. Your station in life is not an excuse. Just "build a better you" through Him who loves you. ✞

NO DIFFERENCE

A Tuskegee Airman being honored

In our nation's War Against Terrorism, great effort is being made by our government to identify individuals who might be suspect of inflicting harm on our innocent citizens. The goal is to bring balance to the screening process of questionable individuals. The opponents to this initiative are screaming out, "This is racial profiling"! There is no question that common sense policy and procedures must be initiated. Yet, we desire to bring no discrimination against the innocent. Our most hallowed document stating "liberty and justice for all," sets the tenor for all of our basic beliefs regarding individual freedom. Unfortunately, in the emotions of war and life-long prejudices, mistakes and injustices have occurred. We must endeavor to avoid these errors in judgments that have occurred in the past. Regardless of the color of skin, race, or religious persuasion, we are reminded time and again that our attitude must be to embrace everyone, for we are a country for all people. As with all "freedoms", there are those who would abuse them to further their own cause or philosophy. We are the great nation "under God" that we are because of our faith, philosophy, and charity. Those who choose to live among us must accept these, or they become traitors to the causes that have made us great.

Following the dastardly sneak attack by the Empire of Japan on Pearl Harbor in December, 1941, many U.S citizens had a prejudged notion that everyone who looked like a "Jap" was a traitor to our nation. Even the government took this stance. Just about every oriental-looking individual was taken from his home and sent to a detention camp. Families were separated, some were sent to camps as far away as South America. Most of these people were Americans, some naturalized and others by birth. They were law-abiding citizens who paid their taxes and voted. Yet, their normal lifestyle was interrupted for the duration of the war because of prejudice.

There was a young man selected to attend the United States Military Academy. His father was an officer in the U.S. Army. The son graduated 35th in the class of 1936. Throughout his four years at the Academy, no cadet ever spoke to him other than on official business. He wanted to fly but segregation was a barrier. Benjamin Oliver Davis, Jr. was the first black graduate of West Point. His father was one of two black combat officers in the entire Army. Finally, when prejudice was set aside, Davis was allowed to enter pilot training and he earned his pilot's wings at Tuskegee Army Base in March, 1942. He was given command of the first all-black unit, the 332nd Fighter Group. They called themselves the Tuskegee Airmen. He led the 99th Pursuit Squadron from Tuskegee to North Africa and later to Sicily. Throughout the war, this unit established a dazzling record of victories against superior German forces. Their exemplary service opened the way for other black units to be formed. In 1954, Davis earned his first star and became the first black general in the Air Force. He served a distinguished career and retired a four star general. Prejudice did not defeat him.

On a recent visit to a beautiful northwestern city, I was drawn to the wording on a plaque beneath the statue of the man who had donated the land for a beautiful park. I found it timely considering current world events. It invites all of us to enjoy the beauty of nature, but more importantly, to recognize the uniqueness of God's creation, our fellow travelers on this earth. Each one is unique and each is worthy of our love and respect. We cannot afford the luxury of prejudice or hatred. This will destroy us. The words which were very meaningful to me read as follows: **"To the use and enjoyment of People's of all colors, creeds, and customs for all times, I name thee Stanley Park."** ✞

THE DESIGN

The clerk at the photo-finishing counter handed an enlarged picture to an elderly gentleman. As he examined it, a younger customer looked on and exclaimed, *"and what is that?"* Obviously, the male questioner with his tattoos, surly smirk, and the sarcastic inflection in his voice was displeased with what he was seeing. The gray-haired gentleman calmly remarked, *"That is the scene of a World War II heavy bomber raid on a munitions factory in Germany." "And I suppose you will tell me that you were in that airplane right there?"* he said pointing to a four engine heavy bomber... *"killing people without just cause.?" "No, I was not in that aircraft. Had I been, I would not be here talking to you, for that crew perished." "And,"* the veteran continued, *"had not that crew along with thousands of other brave Americans given their lives, you would not be standing here either. Their lives were the price that was paid for your freedom."*

The men who fought in WWII came from a vast reservoir of American decency. Their sense of duty compelled them to fulfill their honor and destiny. American society is still called upon to produce this kind of men who would step forth to serve, sacrifice, suffer, and if necessary, die. One of our recent wars, called Desert Storm, verified that men like this are indeed among us.

The Great Designer has a purpose for every life. It takes many years for the purposes of some individuals to be fulfilled, while others fulfill theirs in a very short period of time. All lives, whether long or short, affect others. ***"For none of us lives to himself alone and none of us dies to himself alone." (Romans 14:7 NIV)***

The ultimate goal of life is eternal life. Regardless of how many years man lives, life is short in comparison to eternity. From the beginning of life until the end, there will be conflict and resulting battle scars. Are you satisfied with what you are doing with your life? If not there is still time to make a change. And after that, the trip... ✞

Bombs away, On Target

MAKE A DIFFERENCE

Do you remember the name of the teacher who was your most favorite? At what age were you when this teacher came into your life? What was the subject matter? How did this teacher make a difference in your life?

Interesting enough, all of us have had a teacher in our lives with a common name. We have had instruction geared to our individual needs coming at a time when we least expected it but always there, teaching us. What is this teacher's name? _Life Itself._ The subject matter is as varied and different as we are. We are bombarded with information and experiences from the beginning of our life until we take our final breath. Life experiences have given more joys and astonishments than sorrows and disappointments. We all have known good and evil, love and hatred, compassion and anger, acceptance and rejection, happiness and pain, successes and failure. Considering the ups and downs we experience, "life itself" is our greatest teacher and gift.

Prime Minister Winston Churchill, the motivator, the teacher

Teachings come through the experiences of life. Every day presents an incredible opportunity regardless of who we are. As a result, life can be a great and worthwhile event under difficult times. Under the worst of circumstances, Winston Churchill, Britain's war-time Prime Minister, spoke on 18 June 1940, the following often quoted statement…"Men will still say, 'this was their finest hour." This was not a fine hour for Britain, in fact it was a dark hour for not only England but for the civilized world. Germany's juggernaut of military might had conquered the lowland countries and France had fallen into their hands. The British Expeditionary Force had thousands of troops deployed, the French had a smaller number of troops committed, and a German spearhead broke down all military resistance. These forces were trapped and were at the mercy of Nazi Panzer Divisions. The Battle of Dunkirk followed. The Free Encyclopedia Wikipedia describes the action: Operation Dynamo was the name given to the mass evacuation during the Battle of Dunkirk conducted from May 26, 1940 to June 4, 1940 under the command of Vice –Admiral Bertram Ramsay from Dover. In nine days, 338,226 French and British soldiers were taken from Dunkirk, France and the surrounding beaches by a quickly assembled fleet of about seven hundred vessels. These craft included the Little Ships of Dunkirk, a mixture of merchant marine vessels, fishing boats, pleasure craft and RNLI lifeboats, whose civilian crews were called into service for the emergency. Though the "Miracle of the Little Ships" is a major folk memory in Britain (at the time a useful propaganda tool), over 80% of the troops evacuated embarked from the Harbour's protective mole onto the 42 destroyers and other larger ships participating in the operation.

Churchill's address to Parliament came only days after the Battle of Dunkirk. Following this were the attacks of the German Luftwaffe air-blitzkrieg of London and the industrial cities of Britain. The Prime Minister faced opposition and lost support of his Cabinet and there was fear that he might be replaced by Lord Halifax who favored a negotiated peace. However Churchill, the teacher, did not give up. His resolve buoyed British moral when he declared, *"Britain and the British Empire will fight on, if necessary for years, if necessary alone."*

In his final remarks to the House of Commons on 18 June 1940 he declared to this audience and to the free world as well his teachings and convictions.

I expect that the Battle of Britain is about to begin.   Upon this battle depends the survival of Christian civilization. Upon it depends our own British life, and the long continuity of our institutions and our Empire. The whole fury and might of the enemy must very soon be turned on us. Hitler knows that he will have to break us in this island or lose the war. If we can stand up to him, all Europe may be free and the life of the world may move forward into broad, sunlit uplands. But if we fall, then the whole world, including the United States, including all that we have known and cared for, will sink into the abyss of a new Dark Age made more sinister, and perhaps more protracted, by the lights of perverted science. Let us therefore brace ourselves to our duties and so bear ourselves that, if the British Empire and its Commonwealth lasts for a thousand years, men will still say , "This was their finest hour."

He declared, "I see great reason for intense vigilance and exertion but none whatever for panic or despair." At this time, the Germans had conquered a large part of the Western Europe coastline. The Nazi's had overrun France and many small neighboring countries. The possibility of intense air attacks against the British Isles and the threat of German submarines sinking, almost at will, the boats carrying life sustaining food and war materials for this nation was a grim reality. Yet, the British leader said; "We are pushed to continue the war."

At this moment in history, England stood alone. There were those who favored capitulation but Churchill was inflexible. He had the resolve to continue the war and win it. He was the teacher of the moment. The teachings of one man rallied the Free World. His life had not been an easy one. "Life itself" had been his teacher. ☩

HAPPINESS ATTAINABLE

It has been said, "Change is often desirable, frequently necessary, and always inevitable." But I would suggest some things never change. For instance, happiness is in constant demand - we all need it. When describing

a happy child, we believe that his most pleasant memories center around his playmates, his school experiences and teachers, being with mom and dad, and receiving praise for something well done. This is a happy time for him. A parent is happiest when love is practiced among all family members, there is a congenial atmosphere, there is comfortable housing for the family, food in the pantry and the family members are healthy. A happy moment comes for an airman after having been in battle and on a difficult

Relaxing airmen, Punting, (a type of boating), a favorite pastime on the River Cam, Cambridge, England

mission for a long period of time over enemy territory. Suddenly he realizes he is almost home. His aircraft is gradually descending toward the home field and then, the pleasant squeal of the tires as his aircraft touches the runway. Happiness is when this same airman sees his "buddy's" aircraft has also landed safely. Both of them can chalk up another combat mission and they are one mission closer to finishing their tour and going home.

There are many phases of life through which all of us pass. Aldous Huxley is quoted as having said: *"Happiness is not achieved by the conscious pursuit of happiness; it is generally the by-product of other activities."* Life is made up of many episodes and although when going through them happiness is not what is perceived, nonetheless it is hidden in that experience to be recognized only later. The Veterans have spent their youthful years and the war is behind them. Marriage followed for some and for years many existed on a "shoestring." Houses, sometimes sub-standard in quality, became their homes. Early on, there were financial difficulties, successful careers were slowly achieved and finally, working years were behind. Families are on their own, days of punching the clock are over, retirement funds are coming in. Maintaining reasonably good health is a challenge. What have we learned? What have life's experiences taught us? What Legacy can we pass on to our children and grandchildren?

We have had the privilege of living in an interesting era. Many Presidents have passed through Washington, D.C. Politicians come and go. Corporations rise and fall. Wars are a constant reminder that there are power-hungry self-appointed individuals always keeping the world in turmoil. With all of the negative forces attacking us from every angle, many would lead us to believe that happiness is unattainable. Perhaps we are looking for it in the wrong places. Recorded in Biblical history, King Solomon declared that man attains happiness through wisdom and understanding. From the 1940's the war years to the present - time and experiences have taught us a few things. (1) Pass on money and it spoils. (2) Pass on power and it corrupts. (3) Pass on knowledge and it breeds haughtiness. (4) Pass on beauty and it breeds pride. In fact, the true legacy that is passed on to humankind is intangible. To pass on happiness we cannot do. That is up to the individual. But it is demonstrated through intangible traits such as love, morality, character, decency, compassion, kindness and a good name. These are the qualities that I experience when I meet with the "happy warriors", fliers, ground crew members and support teams of the 1940's.

"Happy is the man who finds wisdom, And the man who gains understanding; For her proceeds are better than the profits of silver, And her gain than fine gold...and all the things you may desire cannot compare with her. Length of days is in her right hand, In her left hand riches and honor." (Proverbs 3:13, 14, 16 NKJ) ✝

Airmen at leisure

WAR AND PEACE

War is a horrible thing, but loss of freedom is even worse. How do we as Americans view our loyalty, citizenship and love for country? There are those who take our citizenship for granted and fail to realize the beauty, liberty and freedom we enjoy everyday. These are the losers in our society. The majority of our citizens are not like this. We have, as a Nation, demonstrated a fighting spirit to preserve freedom, not only for ourselves, but also for the peace-loving people throughout the world.

In our own history, we sent millions of white men into battle, made tens of thousands of our citizens homeless, destroyed farms and industry, and crippled the infrastructure of our nation to free millions of black men. Later our nation was thrust into a world-wide war, we sent millions of men to Europe and the Pacific at great cost in resources and the lives of our youth, won the war and then taxed ourselves to pay for the rebuilding of these defeated nations. Later Communism began invading the nations of the world, spreading their doctrine of greed and domination. To overcome their threats, we engaged ourselves in what was called the Cold War to defeat their goal of world dominance. Again, we taxed ourselves to help restore freedom and liberty in those oppressed nations throughout the world. Has, ever in human history, another nation in the world done this?

We have not been an aggressive nation but we have been, nevertheless, engaged in almost all world-wide conflicts. While America enjoyed relative peace in October of 1939, only 16.8 percent of Americans favored entering into the war that was simmering in Europe. The politicians were willing to help the allied war effort but in July, 1941, only 14 percent were willing to declare war. However, when we were attacked in December, 1941, we were suddenly willing to step up and defend our freedom. Just prior to the declaration of war with Germany and Japan, 71 percent of all Americans favored a bill requiring mandatory drafting of its citizens to build our fighting forces. For the next four years, 1942-1945, recruiting men for an army was not the problem, training and equipping them was. America was not only able to mobilize but also willing to meet the challenge of becoming the "arsenal of democracy" for the free world. In the end, mobilized civilians supplied the food and wartime materials to support our military force of twelve million men and also helped to feed and arm all of our allies. The staggering price was the 400,000 American fighting men who died in the war.

Until our freedom was challenged in the early 1940's, America wanted to stay out of the war. It was Europe's war. The killing of Jews, Frenchmen, Englishmen, Russians was "not an American problem". But, when our freedom was challenged, everything changed! The consequences of indifference were very clear. The goals and aspirations of the citizens of the United States were threatened. We understood that whenever our freedoms are challenged, we must act! The love for our great nation must be understood by everyone and is worthy of defending. When you don't love something, you lose it.

Our nation has too many ungrateful people with an eye on a "What's in it for me?" attitude. Ours is the greatest nation in the world and people throughout the world have a strong desire to come to America, join us, and become a citizen of the U.S.A. Unfortunately the vocal minority in our Nation are "getters", not "givers", but still it is a Nation made up of people who have an honest appreciation and gratitude in their hearts. Without this love for America, we begin to lose what we hold dear. God made this a very special place, whose streets are not paved with gold but rather with golden opportunities. Our war-time leader, President Franklin D. Roosevelt, spoke, of these as "four essential human freedoms", the protection of which is our nations great calling: (1) Freedom of Speech, (2) Freedom of Worship, (3) Freedom from Want, and (4) Freedom from Fear.

Those who have gone before - the Patriots, Statesmen, Veterans, Citizen Soldiers and all unnamed heroes - have paid the supreme price. *This is the price that was paid for the privilege I have of being alive today!* ✝

Winston Churchill, Harry Truman, Joseph Stalin; world leaders near the end of WWII

ARE YOU PRAYING?

In a moment of crisis, people cry out to a power that is beyond them. Repeated over and over are stories about men who prayed for their own safety: when things were out of control, when enemy fighters dotted the sky around them, when an engine was on fire, when the smell of cordite from exploding shells penetrated their aircraft, when survival seemed impossible. After the battle and when the aircraft and crew were back home and on solid ground, there was some jesting just to "let off steam." A common remark was: "*I just bet the Lord heard a lot of strange voices over the target today.*" This is probably so! Someone surmised that "there was more praying done by the members of the aircrews on missions than the combined prayers of all of the armed forces chaplains in the European theater.

I have been in the company of a man, who in a modest manner, told of his own blood brother who has risen to great heights in their church, and parents who take great pride in the fact that their son is studying for the Priesthood, and others whose mother or grandmother was a person of prayer. We welcome this spiritual boost. But we shy away from the idea of personal prayer until crisis comes. God likes to hear from us whether things are right or wrong. And God the Father, like a doting parent, is glad and willing to take whatever He can get from us in the way of prayer, or praise, or worship or any combination of these. He really welcomes our approach.

As old airmen get together, we realize that time may be running out for us and we are more willing to admit our humanity. We feel the need to confess emptiness in our spirit. We begin to welcome prayer and participate in it. Let it continue to be repeated with greater intensity and frequency in our lives. Let's learn together to interact in depth with God and each other. If we take the first step, and it may be at the Kindergarten level, let's keep it up. We are learning.

"Let us therefore come boldly to the throne of grace, that we may obtain mercy and find grace to help in time of need." (Hebrews 4:16 NKJ) ✞

How About It?

SURPRISES

"When I die, I want to go like my grandfather did." "How is that?" his friend asked. "Peacefully, in his sleep. I sure don't want to die screaming and yelling like all of the passengers in his car!"

Well, life is like that. It is full of unexpected events, the elements of surprise, the unpredictable phases of life that slip up on us so very speedily. First birth, then infancy, followed by childhood, adolescence and adulthood with marriage and its many adjustments. Following are the hassles of employment and involvement with the corporate world, the raising of a family, and bill paying. At this age, the title of "sandwich generation" often applies. Life is sandwiched in between our children and later their children who need guidance and in all likelihood financial assistance. About the same time, there is the care of aging parents with their many needs.

Following the "sandwich generation" phase, the status of Senior Adult is achieved. Now, an exercise is entered into called "retirement". The person who has speedily gone through all of the above facets of life and announces his retirement suddenly feels like he has moved into Utopia. However, after a few days or perhaps a few weeks later, without a plan of action for the rest of life, routine events can turn into sheer boredom. If each day is without physical, mental and spiritual goals, life can become a drag. Each new sunrise brings the tasks of dressing, eating, and routine household chores which can drive us to a condition called "cabin fever." When this happens, we often ask "What has happened to me? Years have just zipped by. Where did the time go anyway?" An anonymous writer explained it in this manner...

> **"Life is just a minute**
> **Only sixty seconds in it,**
> **Forced upon you, can't refuse it.**
> **Didn't seek it, didn't choose it,**
> **But it's up to you to use it.**
> **You must suffer if you lose it,**
> **Give account if you abuse it,**
> **Just a tiny little minute,**
> **But eternity is in it."**

All of us have been given dreams that came from God. Some have not yet been achieved. They are gifts and our goals are precious. They cannot be ignored. We must honor them. It is easy to look back and say, "What if?" Do you drive your car by looking in the rear-view mirror for your frame of reference instead of forward where you are going? Of course not! Memories (looking back) are precious, we love them but the past will not help us fulfill our dreams of today. We must forever be alive to conditions and folks around us now. We are leaving a legacy. After people die, they really do live on through those who love them. ☫

LISTENING

Margaret had made the long train trip from Tennessee to Oregon to be with her husband. Clyde was a B-17 bombardier. His crew was finishing up their phase training and soon his outfit would be shipping out to an overseas assignment. He and Margaret would be together for a short time before saying their final good-bye prior to his combat assignment. Very early on the morning of August 18, 1943, Margaret was standing on the balcony of the old hotel where she was living when in the distance she heard a rumbling explosion and looking up, witnessed a mid-air collision of two B-17's. High in the Oregon sky, one aircraft exploded and the second went into a steep dive. In her frightened spirit, she knew Clyde was involved.

That morning, several aircrews were assigned to a training mission. Before takeoff, Clyde had a strong premonition to put on his parachute. He ignored this "small still voice" speaking to him. Again, he was reminded a second time, "Clyde, you did not put on your parachute." This time he listened! Twenty minutes later, the collision happened! The impact threw Clyde from the wreckage. His parachute was badly damaged by fire but he successfully descended, the only survivor of twenty men. Almost immediately, the driver of a jeep picked him up. They drove over the rough terrain and eventually found a telephone. By the time he called the base operations, Margaret had run the entire distance from the hotel and was standing in base operations when his telephone message arrived. Clyde identified himself and said, "I have been in a bad accident." The young WAAC operator with whom he was speaking responded by saying, "There were no survivors!" Clyde did not argue with her for he knew better. The operator did say however, that a young woman was standing in the office in tears. On the phone with her, Clyde said four words, "Margaret, I made it!"

Clyde believes, as I do, that his obedience to that "small still voice" was the difference between life and death.

God is not a cosmic bellboy for whom we can press a button and get our way. God has placed in us a conscience. . .His presence in us. This He uses to speak to us! He did not create us to be robots. We determine our destiny by the obedience we exercise in Him.

Clyde listened and obeyed. Clyde and Margaret enjoyed a full and happy life living in a small Tennessee town. Listening made the difference. **"My sheep recognize my voice, I know them, and they follow me." (John 10:27 NLT)** God is still talking! Are you listening and following? ✟

Listening and obeying, Clyde White 50 years later

UNKNOWN AIRMAN

The envelope I received via U.S. mail was mingled in among all of the unwelcome advertising flyers, a magazine or two, pleas for donations, announcements about weddings, graduations, babies, and the usual assortment of "things" which show up in my mail box. I was totally amazed that the postman was able to deliver the only letter that was directed to my attention. It was addressed to "The Chaplain" with my street address and city, hand written by a man, obviously as old as I. His penmanship skills were similar to mine. . . rather hard to read! The caption on the letterhead of

A determined patriot: Winston Churchill

the envelope gave the name of a Veterans Home Board in a certain city and state. This gentleman, Joel, (not his real name), had printed his name above the organizational address with his ballpoint pen, followed by the number of his assigned quarters. Out of curiosity, I checked with the Membership Records Manager at our 8th AFHS National Office. No record of him existed in any of the current or historical membership files. Who was this man? I opened the envelope looking for a letter. The only item inside was a very old and worn one dollar bill. There was no written note or message. Or was there?

Joel, apparently was one of our men. Why did he send a message to me "The Chaplain"? Without question, he was one of the 350,000 men assigned to the 8th Air Force stationed in war- torn England during WWII. Was he one of the ground echelon men or was he an air crew member flying combat missions over enemy territory? I don't know and probably never will. But his message is this: "I am here. . . thinking about you and our time together over there".

Whether Joel is facing financial problems, or physical difficulty, or loneliness, or is without family or anyone to love him, we do not know. But this we know, there are a few thousand surviving Veterans still around. We attend reunions, do hangar flying, and still spin our stories that we have told time and again. And, by and large, we are very grateful for life. But we must not overlook those less fortunate, those in situations similar to Joel.

A godly man was asked, "What do you want on your tombstone1?" He replied, "I want it to read, **He did what he couldn't**". This little quote is true for Joel and all of us. *We couldn't do it but we did.* And all of us must remember to honor and remember those who are out of sight as Joel is, just as we honor and respect one another.

Winston Churchill, Britain's wartime Prime Minister, was one who in his lifetime faced a few victories and many defeats. He was remembered by defining democracy, "*You win some; you lose some.*" Anthony Eden, Churchill's young ally commented about Churchill, "*Courage for some sudden act, maybe in the heat of battle, we all respect, but there is still rarer courage which can sustain repeated disappointment, unexpected failure, and shattering defeat.*" Churchill had that kind of courage, not for days, but for weeks and months and years. In his opinion, the goal of World War II was "*to revive the status of man.*" His ambition was to lift individuals above the Hitlers and Stalins of this world. His life stands as an example of what a free man can be. This is true for all of the Joels out there and all of us, for **we did what we couldn't.**

✝

TRUE GREATNESS

Immediately following the tragic terrorist attacks of September 11, 2001 on New York City, Washington, D.C. and Pennsylvania, there was a resurgence of patriotism and spiritual fervor across our nation. Stores could not stock enough "stars and stripes" flags to meet the demand and churches were crowded with people, some showing grief while others demonstrated a sense of devotion and respect to God for His divine intervention. Within weeks the number of flags diminished and as one pastor said, "The congregation has returned to normal." On the first anniversary of 9-11, there were parades; memorial services, more flags, patriotic gatherings, military aircraft flyovers, and prayers were again initiated. Why?

Americans love their freedoms, freedoms that embrace and include the most loyal and dedicated citizens as well as those who use this liberty to espouse their own selfish agenda in opposition to the goal of "liberty and justice for all." These malicious individuals range from the highest echelons of business and government to the cell-groups designed to destroy the very foundations under which they are privileged to live. American freedom-loving individuals demonstrate their gratitude by cheering, by singing patriotic songs, by consoling the bereaved, by shedding tears, and by showing great pride in recognizing and supporting those of the armed services and other service-oriented organizations. But the one symbol representing all of this is our American Flag. In 1949 President Harry Truman recognized the importance of our national icon and proclaimed June 14th as Flag Day. Earlier in our history, President Calvin Coolidge reminded the nation of the true meaning of the flag when he said, *"When we look at our flag and behold it emblazoned with all our rights, we must remember that it is equally a symbol of our duties. Every glory that we associate with it is a result of duty done. A yearly contemplation of our flag strengthens and purifies the national conscience."*

Ours is a magnificent land with its alabaster cities, towering mountains, sparkling rivers, fertile fields, rich mines and vast fleets carrying its products throughout the world. Its matchless constitution and government "of the people, by the people and for the people" is peerless among the nations of the world. Our schools educating all children, its colleges and universities and its countless thousands of churches teaching, preaching, declaring and encouraging righteousness are all a part of its true greatness. America is great because she is good. If we fail her, she will cease to be great.

Our greatness is measured by the goodness of its citizens. When there is tragedy, an automatic and spontaneous outpouring of concern and compassion results. In simple day-to-day efforts, volunteers seek to make life easier for those in need. When threatened as a nation, her people step forward and unselfishly answer the call. America is a precious gift to the world that is built upon the talents of her people. America has been blessed and she, in turn, blesses the world.

President Theodore Roosevelt, one of our great Presidents, described in his swashbuckling style what was essential to him and to us in achieving goodness and peace.

He said:

"After a week of perplexing problems it does so rest my soul to…come into the house of The Lord and to sing and mean it, "Holy, Holy, Holy, Lord God Almighty" …(my) great joy and glory, that, in occupying an exalted position in the nation, I am enabled to preach the practical moralities of The Bible to my fellow-countrymen and to hold up Christ as the hope and Savior of the world."

This truth is what made President Roosevelt so greatly respected, our country exalted among the nations of the world and us as blessed citizens of the land of our birth. We are a Christian Nation that tolerates all other religions and schools of thought. But we must not forget this historic fact; we have been blessed by Almighty God because we are a Christian nation. ✞

One Nation, Under God

CHOICES AND CHALLENGES

The competition is always keen among airlines. I heard this story that verifies the fact that airlines will go out-of-the-way to keep passenger business. At mid-point in a flight, passengers and baggage were being transferred to another aircraft. Working at a feverish pace the ground crew was sorting baggage and other items when one worker noticed an animal crate, but something was amiss. Inside was a dog. . .the dog was motionless. . .it was dead! The chief in charge of operations saw it and summoned a supervisor. Soon the "company brass" was on the scene. Something like this was unthinkable. A solution had to be found.

Frantic calls were made ahead to the destination of the owner and the animal. The arrival time was over three hours away. There was time to work, and work they did! Animal shelters and pet shops in the next city were contacted until a dog exactly like the deceased animal was found. The markings, sex, size, age were perfect. When the aircraft landed, the replacement animal was rushed to the incoming aircraft, the swapping of the new critter with the old was quickly accomplished and the animal's cage moved nicely along to the baggage claim area. Baggage handlers, flight attendants, pilots, supervisors, were in on the ploy and secretly were very proud of their accomplishments. But, when the female owner appeared to retrieve her baggage and dog, she took one look at the cage and exclaimed to the claims attendant, "That's not my dog."

How could she have known? The surprised attendant asked her to repeat her statement. "That is not my dog" she emphatically declared. The attendant in his most political, diplomatic and polished manner said, "You say this is not your dog? How can you be so sure?" The owner replied instantly." That is not my dog; my dog was dead!"

Life's journey presents us with many challenges. When life begins, we have no choice over our race, family background, our sex, or what our opportunities will be. We are packaged for life. Of course, we have choices and challenges but there are influencing factors throughout life, many over which we have no control. We have our "take-off" and in the span of a few short decades, we reach our final destination. There are many people who are in our lives, those who wish us well to help us improve our situation and others who meddle with our affairs, but we determine our destination by the choices we make, the flight plan we follow. Nothing happens by accident. We take no baggage, so we don't have that hassle, but the Master of our eternal life will show up at the "claims area". Two questions surface in my mind: (1) in what kind of condition will He find us at the end of our journey, and (2) will our Master recognize us as His own? The Scripture is emphatic and gives us certainty. "**But God's truth stands firm like a foundation stone with this inscription, 'The Lord knows those who are his.'**" ✝

ON THE HOME FRONT

It was a small congregation in a mid-western town. Over half of those who attended were young couples and teen-agers. Then the Japanese bombed Pearl Harbor, it seemed that overnight the church pews were half empty. We were all dazed by how fast it all happened! Many of the young men volunteered for military service and the more reluctant were soon drafted.

As the initial shock wore off, we all were searching for ways to help in the war effort. Many of the young wives entered training for jobs in the Douglas Aircraft factory and the munitions plant, leaving their jobs as secretaries and clerks unfilled. We younger ones entered the work force at age 15 to become office assistants or store clerks after school hours and on Saturday.

Cynthia Wassom, the wife of the author and the writer of this article

Daily radio broadcasts, newspaper headlines and the letters received from far-away places caused the home front much trauma and anxiety for the welfare of their loved ones in combat.

In the foyer of the church, a large roll of honor was placed that listed the name of each serviceman from the congregation. The doors of the church were left open and prayer meetings were announced. There was a volunteer around-the-clock vigil as daylight, swing, and grave-yard shifts allowing for one continuous prayer meeting.

From early 1942 to August, 1945 the prayer vigil continued and when the last man returned from his military duty, not a single one whose name appeared on the honor roll had been lost! What a lucky coincidence! I do not believe so. These men served in every branch of service and in every theater of the war. One sailor was dumped into the ocean four times, four ships sunk, before he was picked up again by a vessel that finally made it to port. He was the sole survivor of those who abandoned the first ship. There were other harrowing escapes and experiences equal to this. To me, the statement "prayer changes things" is not a religious cliché. Do you know who was praying for you? Thank them and thank God.

It has been declared, *"Thou art the God that doeth wonders: thou hast declared thy strength among the people. . . thy way is in the sea, and thy path in the great waters, and thy footsteps are not known." (Psalms 77:14,17 KJV)* Our response? *"I will praise thee: for thou hast heard me, and art become my salvation." (Psalms 118:21 KJV)* ✝

How About It?

USE WHAT IS LEFT

At the airport and seated on the spectator side of the security check-point were four girls in their late teens. They were awaiting the arrival of an airline flight and a friend. When they saw that my wife and I were senior citizens waiting for someone as well, all of them stood and politely offered us their seats. Over our protest, they insisted, and after they vacated we sat down. There were two seats unoccupied. We looked over the gathering crowd, spotted a guy obviously a senior citizen, and asked him to join us. We facetiously called it the Senior's Section. He was very defensive of this title and informed us that he was barely sixty-five and didn't like being called a senior citizen. SO??? What's the big deal? Look around, if a person is an American, 65 years of age and over, he is a recipient of social security, unless of course he is independently wealthy, and even then, these folks will often sign up for the benefits just like the rest of us.

The Senior population is constantly being bombarded by commercials, urging us to do estate planning and create "nest eggs" for our retirement thus assuring us a Utopian Life in some exotic place. When we reach that magical age and no longer have to 'punch the clock', the dreamer is ecstatic. For a few weeks life is glorious, that is until boredom sets in. The guy at the airport had reached this point in his life and he had no plans for his retirement and was having difficulty handling it. To cope, often excuses are made for doing nothing at all, such as "I am too old", "I don't have any talents", "I can't do it!" "Let someone else do it!" "I've already done my share!"

The following account I credit to Reporter Jack Riemer of the Houston Chronicle. In Lincoln Center, New York City, a concert was performed by the great violinist Itzhak Perlman. As a child, Perlman was stricken with polio. Ever since that early experience, he has walked only with the aid of two crutches. On the occasion of this November 1995 concert, Perlman laboriously made his way to center stage, and as he sat down, he released the clasps on his legs and made himself comfortable. Shortly after the concert began, a string broke on his violin. Silence reigned in that great concert hall, all eyes were on the guest performer. Would he reverse the procedure, exit the stage, get another violin, or get another string to replace the broken one? Instead, he did not move, he paused, closed his eyes for a few moments and then gave a signal to the conductor to begin again. The audience sat amazed, he was playing with only three strings making the musical changes and adjustments that were necessary to complete the score with mastery, passion and skill. When he finished, everyone arose and cheered. Then, Perlman raised his bow and the people became silent. He said softly, "You know, sometimes it is the artist's task to find out how much music you can still make with what you have."

Many areas of loss and disappointments occur in a lifetime. Yet, it is up to us to find out how much music we can still produce with what we have left. And, we are commanded to do so! No one is without talents and instructions are given how to use them…**"From everyone who has been given much, much will be demanded; and from the one who has been entrusted with much, much more will be asked. (Jesus speaking in Luke 12:48 NIV)** What is being asked of us? Not big things, just little things we can do for those in need such as befriending someone by being a tutor, a companion, a friend, a comforter, a confident, an encourager. Organizations need docents, volunteers, lecturers, entertainers, those who can lead. Society needs storytellers, poets and writers. Humanity needs someone who will pray. Henry J. Van Dyke expressed it well when he said, *"Use the talents you possess, for the woods would be very silent if no birds sang except the best.."* ✝

MAGICAL MOMENT

Our time on earth is spent a moment at a time. Moments come to us automatically and with regularity, one after another with no effort on our part and they disappear just as quickly. A simple errand we are called upon to perform often turns out to take a moment or an hour or perhaps a half a day. This simple task can turn out to be nothing more than a moment killer. As a result, these moments are used up and we become frustrated at our loss of them for they are forever gone.

Everyone has legitimate goals and specific events set for himself that are scheduled to occur later on. This is good! But what about the moments spent while we wait for and anticipate that "magical moment" which is coming up sometime in the future? Those who wait for their "special moment" may never have it but those who find life in the moment-at-hand will discover that their moment is here, at this very time!

Aging is a process that is immediately attached to everyone when they are born. Proud parents record in their memory baby's first smile, first step, first tooth, first scratch, first haircut until these precious moments total up to a twelve month period and the "magical moment" of the one-candle birthday cake. This appears to the child in the photographic record of his life. Of course, the child does not remember this celebration but as candles are added to the cake, the child becomes "hooked on this aging process" and looks forward to the next big celebration.

Like it or not, aging celebrations do occur along the way. There is usually a cake, some gifts, perhaps a card from some long-lost or almost forgotten relative. The 21st birthday seems to stand out as important. I spent mine on the flight deck of my B-24 aircraft in France, guarding it from possible sabotage should a prowling German patrol appear. There was no cake that night. Half-a-century, 50 years spent in this world, seemed like a good time to celebrate. So, two hundred or so people decided to give a surprise party for the Boss. I was somewhat aghast at their enthusiasm over my age accomplishments. Now it was really a surprise when my children, grandchildren, their peers, and friends gathered when I hit 80. They caught me completely off guard. Their greetings I could hear in spite of my weakened sense of hearing, but visual impact was unbelievable. With that many candles, it looked like a fire bomb had been set off, a real smoke-alarm activator.

A prophetic but truthful word was spoken by one of the youngest present at my 'celebration'. "Grandpa" she innocently remarked, "you're so old." Talk about a wake-up call. I realized once again, that it was impossible to kick the habit of aging. The alternative to old age we do not like to talk about! I determined that although more birthdays may come, I will take life one day at a time and relish that "magical moment" when it is given to me. James the Apostle addressed the idea of the "magical moment" when he said, . . . "whereas you do not know what will happen tomorrow. For what is your life? It is even a vapor that appears for a little time and then vanishes away." (James 4:14 NKJ) ✝

AN UNCOMMON LANGUAGE

Babylon has been around a long time and it has been making the headlines for centuries. It's sordid history dates back for thousands of years. One occasion in its early history has impacted the entire world and its occupants ever since. While excavating the original site of the Tower of Babel, archeologists uncovered an ancient tablet verifying the fact that indeed this ancient city existed. The Biblical account tells that these arrogant leaders decided to build a structure that would reach to the heavens, a symbol of their vanity and a monument to their greatness. They had as their goal to reach heaven on their own self-serving terms, but God intervened and brought the project to a halt by confusing the language of the builders. The construction workers could no longer communicate with each other and in their frustration, the builders scattered, taking their new "languages" with them. At that time, the people of the world consequently became multi-lingual and the language barrier has thwarted civilization ever since.

These historic and existing language barriers were not enough. Modern wartime commanders never wanted their orders intercepted and understood by the enemy so their messages were further coded. Human ingenuity of enemy forces however, was able to decode even the most complex system. The process of coding and decoding strategically important messages took time and timing is always an essential element for commanders in the field. An ingenious plan was introduced to speed communication without a breech in security. Some Native Americans who called themselves the Navajo Code Talkers. were brought together during World War II. The Code Talkers used their own Navajo language to communicate military orders quickly and openly among commanders in the field. The complex nature of the Navajo language baffled even the most experienced linguists. The Japanese, who were skilled code breakers, remained baffled throughout the war by these Americans who transmitted messages in their native language openly by telephone and radio. This was a Code that the Japanese never broke.

There is also a common spiritual language that those of faith understand. It is an unbreakable Code that can be understood only by those who have heard the still small voice of God. It is introduced, learned and forged in the heat of battle. Here, even atheists are made aware of the mystery of this Code. Warriors in harm's way often become acquainted with the giver of the Master Code. They have had experiences that are beyond the range of the comprehension of unbelievers. They have a common spirit. War has compelled them to gaze upon the waste and carnage of battle. Everywhere about them is the reality of man's failure and evil intent. Spilt blood and the destruction of war is proof of faulted humanity. There is, however, a common language learned and understood by soldiers through the ages. Despite the reality of the world, they have looked to God who quietly revealed, opened and communicated another world to them, a spirit life, a kingdom that would have no end not built by mankind's effort but by the Spirit of God and forged in the hearts of men. A very wise man living centuries ago best described this Spirit when he said:

"God is our refuge and strength, a very present help in trouble. Therefore we will not fear though the earth be removed, and though the mountains be carried into the midst of the sea; though the waters thereof roar and be troubled, though the mountains shake with the swelling thereof. There is a river the streams whereof shall make glad the city of God, the holy place of the tabernacles of the most High. God is in the midst of her; and she shall not be moved: God shall help her, and that right early. The heathen raged, the kingdoms were moved: He uttered His voice, the earth melted. The Lord of hosts is with us. The God of Jacob is our refuge...Be still and know that I am God". (Psalms 46 1-7, 10 KJV) ☩

A U.S. Marine Navajo Code Talker

PIONEERING SPIRIT

Today, when recognized as a "pioneer pilot", by those much younger, I feel honored. I was never a barnstormer pilot but as a youngster, I was a "pioneer spectator". Early in the century, the airplane symbolized danger and adventure and I watched in awe and amazement as those early flyers performed their daring feats. They loved the showmanship but they also took the risks to raise money to support their aviation adventures. Every mishap or crash, and there were many of them, only added to the fame of this privileged few. The air races conducted in their noisy but flimsy aero planes caused my eyes to dance with excitement as they roared past our prairie homestead farm at tree top level and breath-taking speeds. At one of their shows, I took my first airplane ride and it cost my dad fifty cents. After that, I was hooked. The cow pasture near our house became a landing field from which they operated. I actually got to talk to these daring young men who "risked life and limb" to be innovators, gamblers, and dreamers for early aviation. I heard about Charles Lindberg, but when Wiley Post landed his white Lockheed monoplane, the Winnie Mae, at our local airfield, I actually stood near him and heard his voice. I recall the black patch covering one of his eyes and I remember reading all of the strange sounding names printed on the side of his plane listing the cities and countries he had visited on his around-the-world flight. These pioneers were our mentors and we learned valuable lessons from them.

Warriors of the past at a recent reunion

World War II broke out and tens of thousands of teen-agers were destined to become next generation pioneer pilots. In the early 1940's , we served in the 8th AF in the European Theatre flying out of England. But, the pioneering spirit was kept alive at the end of that military conflict. Man wanted to fly faster, further, higher, safer and in more comfort. The jet airplane was built, pressurized cabins were developed, the sound barrier was broken, space travel was introduced. Man walked on the moon, aviation military strength became awesome, and commercial flights traveling near the speed of sound at high altitudes carrying hundreds of passengers have become common place. The men who were teenagers back in the 1940's have witnessed all of this and have become a part of the legacy of flight.

All of these pioneers are regarded by many as heroes. We admire their accomplishments but we must not forget that they were humans with the common characteristics of the human race. New challenges brought excitement, an increase in adrenalin flow and often great fear. When circumstances found them at the "end of the rope," the final alternative was to reach out to a higher power. If we will really be truthful, the punch line of all the activities of our life is this: *We will at some time in our life, reach the end of ourselves.*

Humanity often acts strangely toward God: our arrogance is met with His patience, our denial with His assurance, our guilt with His forgiveness. When the Almighty is cursed and accused for all of "the bad things" that have happened, He remains faithful. When we desperately desire to know if this "God thing" is real, He is there. We must realize that we are never alone. The song writer describes man's dilemma with these words, *"…without Him, I can do nothing, without Him, I'd surely fail. "* The hope is found in His word, **"With man it is impossible, but with God, all things are possible (Mark 10:27 KJV)** ✞

---

*"Regardless of who or where we are,
help is only a prayer away."*

DO AND DIE

There have been many changes in my eight decades of living. This was vividly demonstrated when my nine year-old granddaughter interviewed me for a report required for her third-grade class. One requirement was that the interviewee had to be over fifty years old. I met this requirement without question. My answers were to be given like I was nine years old. A sampling of the questions in my interview of one hour were: What games did you play? What was school like? Did you have a color TV? Tell me about your bathroom. What did you eat? What was school like? She didn't understand a lot of things, such as no electricity or running water.

A pastor with three very young children has a fascination for history. When he found out about my involvement in the European Theatre during WW II, my popularity rating increased dramatically. He also had questions, questions that I hadn't considered for a long time. I began thinking again about times past but not necessarily my childhood.

I have had decades to try and sort out what really happened during those youthful months and years of my wartime escapades. Those years of combat and mutual experiences brought about a comradeship that bound total strangers together. It brought men together who would have never met one another under any other circumstance. The changes that have occurred in my comrades and me are unbelievable. The things that happened to us then were just as primitive as the events and living conditions of my childhood. I remember the negatives, the scary things, the goofy things, the stupid things, the daredevil tricks we performed. We often asked ourselves the questions, "What are we doing here? Does our being here mean anything? Are we just wasting our time? Will we ever come out of this alive?" At this point of time in my life, I am comfortable with thinking that what we did probably shortened the war and lessened the loss of lives.

For years I, like thousands of others, buried my experiences and refused to discuss them. Oh, we would talk about the lighter things, but the heavy stuff, it was just forgotten. Then a few of the warriors would get together thinking about the things we dared to do and got away with! Some wrote these experiences down and the rest read what they had written. Then the dialogue began flowing and in later years as we got older, the guys started leaving the good earth to join the squadron in the sky. Then, the talking took on a new dimension as we become even closer and declare, "wow, do you realize what we did?" We started out as amateurs in our new military assignment, we were strangers but during that time, we became family.

And now, we can become a part of a world-wide family brought together by a Friend, one who has taken part in every battle that we have ever fought. He has been with us throughout our childhood, youth, war experiences, and all of the battles of our life. His name is Jesus. To describe His friendship and closeness, He has declared**: "Remain in my love. . .I have told you this so that you will be filled with my joy. Yes, your joy will overflow. I command you to love each other in the same way that I love you. And here is how to measure it—the greatest love is shown when people lay down their lives for their friends." (John 15:9-13 NLT)** ✞

Aviation Cadets; future Pilots, Navigators, Bombardiers

IF ONLY

Walter Cunningham was the astronaut who flew on the first crewed spacecraft, *Apollo* in 1968. In his time, he was justifiably perceived to be a modern day hero. He was looked upon with honor, pride and awe by his countrymen Folks saw him as a true pioneer and jokingly would remark, "What do you propose to do when you grow up?" Others would ask, "Would you do it all over again?" "That is a hard act to follow," they would retort, "What now?" I am certain he would remember and review in his mind the vigorous training and the qualifications he had to possess to even be considered for the program, the competition he faced from among the others who desired the appointment, the screening and the sifting that went on before he got approval from the Space Agency. He willingly sought the appointment knowing well the perils and uncertain challenges. We could never know the mounting pressure upon his body and emotions as the first lift-off occurred, then, the first touch down as he came back into the earth's atmosphere. He had many opportunities to speak and at the age of seventy, he made this statement: *"Don't be one of those souls who says, 'If only I had my life to live over!' Live your life in such a way that once is enough."*

Thanks for the memories, but I wonder who would want to live life all over again. If you will, put yourself again in the flying boots of the 1940-45 war time period. The training, the challenges, the opportunities, the perils, the fears, the day-by-day unknowns, the uncertainty of life we faced continually.

Do you remember flying at 22,000 feet with your oxygen mask on, the temperature down to 40 degrees below zero? Ahead, the target and flak and hundreds and thousands of black puffs, just like a cloud-all you can do is sit there, knowing you've got to pass right through it. Then there is always the possibility of fighters slipping in behind you from a bank of clouds. A ship goes down, no chutes are seen, friends disappear before your eyes. We grieve a little and then go on, "This is war" we muse, and this reality somehow helps us justify our apparent dismissal of this terrible loss. Enemy territory passes beneath and Hell is ahead, and then it is behind us. We see the water of the Channel, friendly territory is ahead and we start down. Our oxygen masks come off, we eat a frozen candy bar, we relax a little but not too much, we remain alert and keep our eyes moving. The skies are crowded with aircraft, the clouds are dense, everyone is fighting to find the airstrip, on the ground red flares glow against the gray fog and drizzle telling the ambulance drivers that someone is wounded. When the engines stop turning, a jeep arrives with the news: "Alert for tomorrow's mission."

Yesterday's gone. Its memories may linger but it can never be repeated. A letter of a young airman to his sister testifies of his hope and trust. *"I believe in God and his power and goodness. I've seen God answer my prayers, and calm my nerves, and give me rest. Always before any mission I pray to God for strength and guidance…I've said nothing about this to anyone. Now, I feel free to tell it, as I have 29 missions behind me and only one to go. I have faith God will go with me in this last one as he has in the past."*

Jesus addressed the idea of the sufficiency of our Heavenly Father in facing the challenges, sorrows, joys, opportunities of each day when He said; ***"So, don't worry about having enough food or drink or clothing. Your heavenly father already knows all your needs, and he will give you all you need from day to day, if you live for him and make the Kingdom of God your primary concern. Don't worry about tomorrow." (Matthew 6:31-34 NLT)*** ✝

In the storm of battle

NOT ALONE

We are a generation that remembers vividly the December 7, 1941 attack on our country by a cunning and malicious enemy. This enemy had powerful leaders (both military and civil), an organized form of government, lethal weapons, an established industrial base, and a cooperative citizenship willing to fight. They were a visible force with which to contend. We also remember 9/11, September 11, 2001, a time when our country was once again maliciously attacked. In this attack (almost 60 years later) our enemy was almost invisible, its leader was hard to identify, impossible to find, was driven by self-motivation to destroy freedom loving peoples, and had a small but dedicated, self-sacrificing band of Maverick followers who were eager to make the ultimate sacrifice for their cause.

Cadet Jason Scott Hope, Air Force Academy

Our country has faced over two hundred years of warring conflict, almost all of which came from without the boundaries of our nation. In every conflict, leaders and followers have stepped forward to ensure victory. The generation previous to mine had those individuals who went to war in Europe to fight "Kaiser Bill" in World War I. Since then, there are heroes of WWII, Korea, Vietnam, Desert Storm, Iraq and other areas of political unrest around the world. We of WW II have many heroes whom we respect and honor. I would mention one who is representative of we 8th Air Force veterans. Recently, one of our commanders joined the squadron in the sky. Lt. General Gerald W. Johnson passed away in September, 2002. He was one of our peers and his record was impressive, his post-war experiences helped create a mighty force for our Nation. We revere his memory.

Today, we have a formidable, dedicated, skilled, and talented cadre of servicemen defending our country. One with whom I have the privilege of his friendship, gave me a glimpse of war time encounters in today's conflicts. He is an Apache helicopter pilot. He has recently seen service in Bosnia. The weapon he had available was the powerful laser guided "Hell-Fire" missile, that he was capable of and did deploy. He is a family man, a dedicated individual and is proud to be called an American.

I met a next generation patriot. He is a 17 year-old senior in High School. He is a member of the ROTC cadet corps. He plans to pursue a military track in his life. When asked why he was following this career, he stated that his grandfather was in the army in WWII, his step–father was in the navy and was a specialist in nuclear power-driven vessels. Since there is a history of military service in his family, he has chosen the military because it is his patriotic desire.

Three generations, all of whom used the existing technology of their day, from the primitive which we deployed during WW II, to the atomic applications of the next generation and to the yet-to-be-developed technology of the future. Regardless of our generation, our responsibility to America is unquestioned. All of our lives have been involved in life changing affairs including such things as taxation, defense, business, social issues, family, education, schools and churches. Our lives have, at one time or another, been involved in most of these.

Our responsibility to country and society is essential and regarded with respect by most. Some view it as a God-given duty. But there is a higher calling that prepares man for his final and eternal destiny. This dedication and responsibility to God, has no alternative. An example of one who lived in difficult times and fought pressure from his peers within his own circle and enemies from without declared,

Father, James; Grandfather James Robert; Retired AF Pilots: Three generations of the Hope Family with the United States Air Force

"If you are unwilling to serve the Lord, then choose this day whom you will serve......But for me and my family, we will serve the Lord." (Joshua 24:15, NLT) ✝

DETOURS

During the early 1940's, more specifically the four years of 1941-1945, over seven million young men, all U. S. citizens, experienced a drastic life-changing experience. They came from a variety of backgrounds, ethnic groups, and international origins. There were those who were rich and those who were not, the privileged and those who were not so favored, those who were well-educated and those who had not had the opportunity, factory workers and farmers, every skin color, married and single. They had to leave home, their families, their personal pursuits to follow a call. In short, they were challenged by a change in their lives, a change in the direction which they were heading; a change in everything to which they were accustomed.

These young men became great because their country needed them. When the security of the nation and the safety of its citizens were threatened by power-hungry, ruthless and selfish dictators, they responded. And they responded in huge numbers. In 1940, just before our country was attacked, the U. S. Army had a cadre of 170,000 men in uniform. They were not an honored organization, they were poorly paid, and they had inadequate training and equipment. Then there was the attack on Pearl Harbor on December 7, 1941 followed a few days later by the declaration of war by Germany. Suddenly the United States was forced into action to become an active player in the conflict that raged throughout the world. It was into this conflict that the seven million young men moved onto the stage

Training for war

of action. One historian described this transition of manpower as follows: *"…General George Marshall had transformed the U.S. Army from a cadre of 170,000 men in 1940 to an army four years later that numbered 7.2 million (2.3 million in the Army Air Force). It was the best equipped, most mobile, with the most firepower, of any army on earth. This achievement was one of the greatest accomplishments in the history of the Republic."*

This accomplishment was not a forced patriotism by society but an individual willingness to give of themselves for a cause. They took a detour in their lives. They took it without regret and received this change with pride and enthusiasm. Without exception, they all griped and complained at the strangeness and inconveniences of the changes that plagued their lives. It was a new life but it brought the best out of them and they, by and large, were pleased in what they were called to do in this new endeavor. Their credo seemed to be: *"The really happy person is the one who can enjoy the scenery when he has to take a detour."*

The detour and the scenery were new. It brought new friends, new skills, new vistas of living, an exposure to sorrow, loss and even death of comrades that no other experience could or would give. But, when the detour ended and they returned back to their previous track of life, they were better men as a result of the trip. Life had greater meaning, and satisfaction and happiness were theirs because of this commitment.   It was not only their personal fortitude and pledge but it was also the work of faith in the Almighty moving in them. Solomon best described this state of life when he said: **"Commit to the Lord whatever you do, and your plans will succeed. The Lord works out everything for his own ends." (Proverbs 16:3-4 NIV)** ✝

After the battle, a reunion at San Diego, California

VOICES

We saw him on international television. He became known after this momentous appearance as "Comical Ali." Broadcasting from a poorly-lighted and drab studio surrounded by a sea of microphones, Iraqi Information Minister Mohammed Saeed ali-Sahaf stood before the cameras and became a sudden TV star. He reported, on behalf of his boss Saddam Hussein, the defeat of the invading collation forces and military units of the United States *"These forces"* he reported, *"have been repelled by the mighty Republican Guard and there is nothing to fear by the Iraqi people."* On other TV channels, with a direct link between the war front and viewers around the world, were the scenes and the sounds of bombs exploding on targets, military tanks, support equipment, and troops moving at will through the streets, not only of Bagdad but other cities in Iraqi as well. Both telecasts were running at the same time but with conflicting reports. The question; did "Comical Ali" lack the proper facts or was he just reporting? Being a public information spokesman, he may have been plagued with what many journalists face. Sometimes there is not much news to report. Perhaps he followed the philosophy: "No news is bad news, good news is dull news, and bad news makes marvelous copy."

Adolph Hitler, Master of Deceit

Through the years, words have been used to influence the actions of people. During WW II, the Germans were masters of deception. One of the first attacks they employed against novice airmen was the use of false radio transmissions to lure newly arriving airmen into enemy territory. Aircraft were directed into the paths of fighter aircraft and some were given false signals to lure them to unfriendly airdromes built specifically to encourage them to land in enemy-held territory. American forces in the European Theatre became accustomed to the voice of Axis Sally and the Brits were acquainted with *Lord Haa Haa*. These two individuals gave out information on the airwaves, some of it extremely accurate and some very deceiving. It was propaganda at its best. The reports were designed to demoralize the listeners. Broadcasts about the men and their military units listed as "Top Secret," were very accurate. How much did the enemy really know? But the gory information about our bombing effectiveness had to be written off as myth. The only good feature of these programs was the airing of popular American music, which we rarely heard. We listened for the music, not the message.

How does one deal with things heard? Throughout life, messages come from many sources. Some ideas are worthy, while others are not. People decide what to believe. Few are neutral. From birth to death, no one is exempt from voices bidding for our lives and influence. Don't limit yourself simply because you are from an obscure place or lowly station in life. God loves to take the least of us and turn us into something great and significant in His eyes. It makes no difference where you are from. All that really counts: Where are you going? Why are you going? Who is going with you? After all, God is never misleading. Connect with Him. Listen to His instructions and follow them. Ignore those messages and voices that are destructively wrong. Listen to what God has to say!

"Each one should use whatever gift he has received to serve others, faithfully administering God's grace in its various forms. If anyone speaks, he should do it as one speaking the very words of God. If anyone serves, he should do it with the strength God provides so that in all things God may be praised through Jesus Christ." (I Peter 4:10-11 NIV) ✝

Hitler's Youth, Following a Myth

GOING HOME

In the last century, there was a very successful gentleman. He had made his fortune honestly. He was well respected by just about everyone. In an effort to show his gratitude to his country and his fellow countrymen, he invested huge amounts of his wealth back into the nation that had given him the opportunity to become an entrepreneur. He became ill and died. Because of his fame and generosity, the news of his death spread and long lines gathered to see his remains and show respect for him and his family. Among the hundreds viewing his casket, one of two men passing by was heard to remark, "I wonder how much he left?" The second responded immediately, "He left it all."

What do we leave and what do we take with us?

The war ended in Europe. Tens of thousands of men assigned to the air crews and the members of the ground echelon stationed in countless airfields across England were idle. The pastoral scene, which existed before the war, returned. The grass was green, the skies were blue, and the silence was eerie in the early spring morning. The Officer of the Day did not make his appearance to awaken the combat air-crews from a fitful sleep. The Hamilton Propellers driven by the powerful twin-row radial Pratt and Whitney engines were not giving off their customary growling and sputtering sounds in the pre-dawn darkness. Trucks and jeeps were idle and the early risers were on their bicycles heading for breakfast at the chow hall. The aircraft sat idle in their revetments. The long lines of aircraft were not lined up along the perimeter getting ready for take-off. The war was over. These weapons of war had finished their assignment. The men who manned them and maintained them were going home.

Now the possibility of death by the enemy was passed. The objects associated with safety and superstitions were brought out into the open. Things thought to bring good luck, well-worn rabbit's feet, four-leaf clovers, horse shoe medallions and the like were now discarded. Many crews had pre-flight rituals that they preformed. One crew never felt good about take-off until the navigator played the official air-force song on his homemade flute. One guy refused to launder his long-john underwear during his entire combat tour. Perhaps the most dramatic expression made by a single person was by the airman who removed his fleece-lined boots and left them on the tarmac and walked away, his expression of finality. All were going home, these things were left behind. There was no further need for them.

The philanthropist left all behind as all of us will do! All of the things that we find significant in this life become meaningless when we face eternity. Once we are home, we get a new set of values. Since we leave everything behind, perhaps we should consider what has lasting value. Solomon, the wisest man who ever lived, leaves us this wisdom. *"Choose a good reputation (name) over great riches, for being held in high esteem is better than having silver or gold. The rich and the poor have this in common, the Lord made them both." (Prov.22:1-2, NLT)* ✝

Homeward Bound

RISK TAKERS

After having been involved in the passing of the Declaration of Independence, John Adams wrote to Abigail Adams, *"I am well aware of the toil and blood and treasure that it will cost us to maintain this Declaration, and support and defend these States. Yet through all of the gloom I can see rays of ravishing light and glory. I can see that the end is worth more than all of the means."* John Adams was both a prophet and a visionary. He had signed on with a small number of patriots who wanted more out of life than that of servitude to a far-away monarch. He knew it would cost something to break away from the foes surrounding the small group of determined patriots occupying regions of this new nation that they had chosen to call the United States. The foes were real. One claimed, and it was true, "that the sun never sets on the British Empire." They maintained a mighty navy and controlled the sea surrounding its vast empire and they had a militia second to none, to maintain stability and provide leadership. Furthermore, they occupied vast regions of land north of this emerging new republic and British troops were readily available to step in and maintain stability for the Throne. Then to the south there was Spain and their Armada of men-of-war ships and their armies. They were willing and anxious to protect all of the lands that they had "discovered" in the New World. They were intent on keeping this territory. To the west, the French "owned" the Mississippi valley and were aware of the riches to be gleaned from it and they were not willing to lie down and give up this exciting and unexplored land. John Adams was correct that it would take toil, blood and money to maintain this Declaration.

The colonists did have to take up arms. Their freedom did cost much. Blood was shed. But their resolve has been unmatched in the annals of history. One example among the many confrontations they had with the British was that of a small contingent of soldier-citizens in East Tennessee and Western North Carolina. The enemy was surging through the rugged but valuable territory of this New Nation when the colonists rose up in defiance against the invading Red Coats. They mustered at Watauga Flats and marched against the enemy. The "King's Mountain Men," as they called themselves, had a credo that matched the spirit of the New Republic: *"They trusted in God and they kept their powder dry."*

In his letter to Abigail, his assessments of this Declaration have been self-full-filling prophecies. *"Through the gloom"* he said, *"there are rays of light and glory"* The end is worth more than all of the means. Our generation and preceding generations have faced the enemy and we have been victorious. It has cost greatly in wealth, in suffering, in lives, in anxiety, in uncertainty, in unrest, in waste. But the end-results have been worth it. America, the beautiful, and the home of the brave. The words of the song express the spirit of America, *"Across the valleys, from the hills and plains, from mountains' majesty, O, hear the strains of freedom's anthem singing freedom's dream: sweet land of liberty, of thee I sing!"* The prophet Jeremiah summed it up when he declared, **"...the Lord liveth, in truth, in judgment and in righteousness, and the nations shall bless themselves in him and in him shall they glory." (Jeremiah 4:2 KJV)** To remain a great nation, we the people, our government, our leadership must continue doing what we did in the beginning, to become the ravishing light of glory our founding fathers envisioned. ✝

TO THE THIRD GENERATION

How very excited we of the 466th Bomb Group were to have our own special "dooley" guest at the annual gala banquet. She was the center of attention and everyone wanted to have his picture taken with this beautiful and charming young lady. And how did this all come to pass? Well, it's an interesting story that had its beginning in July, 1943.

At Victory Field, Vernon, Texas, Wassom had completed his primary flight training (Class of 43K) and D.R. "Duncan" Miller, his flight instructor, was wishing him and his three other student cadets success in their military careers. All of them succeeded, all four finished their Cadet training, were awarded their wings and commissions as second lieutenants, and they went to war, three as B-24 pilots and one as a P-51 pilot. All survived the war and they all had successful civilian careers.

Earl Wassom, Veteran and C4C Kathryn Miller, Air Academy Dooley

Recently, Wassom heard of Duncan Miller's 82nd birthday party and contacted him. In their telephone conversation that day, Miller revealed that his granddaughter was a first year cadet "dooley" at the Air Force Academy. Quick phone calls and arrangements were made and C4C Kathryn "Katie" Miller became one of the invited Air Force Academy Guests to attend the 29th Annual 8th AF Historical Society Reunion Gala Banquet in Colorado Springs on Saturday, October 19, 2003.

It was love at first sight. Wonderful and charming "Katie" was accepted by over fifty 466ers present at the banquet. She brightened up the photos taken with many old Veteran "geezers" and received a hug from Lt. General Bruce Carlson, Commander of the 8th Air Force.

Katie had spent her previous six years in Japan and is fluent in the Japanese language. She also speaks other languages. She wants to be an Air Force pilot. She has already soloed in a J-3 Cub and Cessna 140. Who was her instructor? It was none other than her very proud grandfather, Duncan Miller.

Our generation is still influencing the youth of today. I pray we may be good examples for them to emulate, not only in their career choices, but in moral, character and the patriotic issues in their lives as well. Solomon summed it up when he declared: **_"Train up a child in the way he should go. And when he is old he will not depart from it."_**_(Proverbs 22:6, NKJ)_ ☦

FOCAL POINT

Recently, the sign on a pick-up truck caught my attention. It said, "I Buy Junk". Apparently, the driver was doing all right in his business. The vehicle that he was driving was the latest model. It had a gleaming paint job, extra mirrors, antennas, chrome wheel covers, a sturdy bumper that protected the powerful fog lights behind it. In fact, it was loaded with all of the "extras". Even the lettering of his sign was artfully done. The small print under his sign, I am sure, was composed with a tongue-in-cheek touch of humor. It stated simply, *"We cheat the other guy and pass the savings on to you!"* Now,

Help at the end of a tough mission

this fellow was not only successful but also had a sense of humor and was fully enjoying the life he was living. Junk collecting may not be for you, but this guy had an attitude toward life that could be beneficial to all of us.

So many folks fail to have fun and be thankful in their situation. They just "punch the clock", put in their hours, draw their breath and draw their salary. The only day they enjoy is Friday which is pay day. Now, a lose-lose situation for this kind of person is for him to die before Friday.

There are billions of human beings on this planet. We are all prone to underestimate our worth. But in the midst of the billions of people on earth, God sees and counts each one of us, one by one. Each individual is special in His sight. Why me? Of what use am I in this world? With so many people who have so many gifts and skills who are already doing so many things that are so important, who needs me? With so many overwhelming needs in the world, what can I do to make the society more desirable?

You are *you*---the only *you* in the entire world! You are unique, one of a kind. No one else has the heritage you enjoy. The wide ranges of experiences you have encountered are yours, and yours alone. The precise events, struggles, achievements, blessings, setbacks in your life have shaped your life and have brought you to this moment. Use all these experiences as focal points in your pilgrimage of life. More than likely, there are great needs in your family, the organizations to which you belong or the neighborhood in which you live. Regardless of your age, you can be a helping hand to someone and we all need to be needed. Search out a place of service. It need not be spectacular. The process of helping people is not changed by a crusade, a rally, and a

Remembrance Service, Brits and Vets, All Saints Church at Attlebridge, England

protest march but rather by individuals who, like yourself, have made a difference. Is there a child that needs to be held? Do you know a teen-ager who could use an encouraging word? Have you a friend or acquaintance that is shut in and needs a friend to sit and talk with him? Would a prayer strengthen and encourage him? Are you yourself shut in but have access to a telephone? Perhaps your pastor or a social worker could give you the names of those who need encouragement. Call them. They will appreciate your concern. I have heard that some people will engage a telemarketer in conversation just to have someone with whom they can talk.

Men of example, principle and purity are needed to set the standard in this world where values, morals and integrity are often expressed in vague and apologetic terms. There is someone in every situation that can set the tenor and create an atmosphere of hope and joy. Let us be the optimistic ones.

The Psalmist thousands of years ago gave a model for us to follow. He said, *"This is the day that the Lord has made, let us rejoice and be glad in it." (Psalms 118:24 KJV)* ✞

"Let us learn our lessons. Never, never believe any war will be smooth and easy, or that anyone who embarks on the savage voyage can measure the tides and hurricanes he will encounter. The Statesman who wields to war fever must realize that once the signal is given, he is no longer the master of policy but the slave of unforeseeable and uncontrolled events. Antiquated War Offices, weak incompetent or arrogant Commanders, untrustworthy allies, hostile neutrals, malignant Fortune, ugly surprises, awful miscalculations - all take their seats at the Council Board or on the morrow of a declaration of war. Always remember, however sure you are that you can win, that there would not be a war if the other man did not think that he also had a chance."

Winston Churchill, *In My Early Years*

How About It?

RECOGNITION

Gratitude, appreciation, respect, love… are just a few of the words that have been expressed to the Veterans by the younger generation who recognize the horrors of World War II and the great price that was paid for freedom. In England, decades after the end of the war, a Brit voluntarily approached a visiting Yank and thanked him for his contribution in preserving his freedom and in "saving the world." At the dedication of the World War II Veterans Memorial in Washington D.C., tens of thousands of Veterans of that war were recognized and honored. The younger generation present openly wept and rejoiced with these men and expressed their thanks for the sacrifice they made. In social gatherings and without fanfare, sincere face-to-face expressions of gratitude are not uncommon.

These are humbling experiences. They come unexpectedly. How does a Veteran properly react? Does he try to explain love for family, God and country? Can it be understood that "love takes the sting out of duty"? In the fury of war and without thought, duty and love become one. At the end of the Normandy campaign following D-Day, the Allies had 2,168,307 men armed, trained, and available and most were engaged in combat on what was called the Western Front. On the Eastern Front there were millions of Russians engaged in battle. Of those soldiers, tens of thousands gave their lives on the ground and in the air. Many died but many more survived. The survivors, after 60 years, are still humbled at the accolades they receive for doing what they considered only to be their duty.

Montgomery, the stubborn and opinionated British General, in 1942 assumed command of a beaten and dispirited English Army that had been pushed all over North Africa by the Germans and humiliated by their leader, Field Marshal Erwin Rommel who was given the title, "The Desert Fox". In these circumstances, Montgomery issued a new order, perhaps his most famous. *"We will fight the enemy where we now stand: there will be no withdrawal and no surrender. If we cannot stay here alive, then let us stay here dead!"* Cold blooded? Not really. Monty asserted his leadership. His men entrusted their lives to him. He was a courageous and caring leader and they submitted to his authority. He once asked an infantry soldier what his most valuable possession was. The soldier replied, *"My rifle Sir."* *"No it isn't,"* declared Monty. *"It's your life and I 'm going to save it for you."*

It is not in the large military units where crises and danger are overcome, but rather by acts of individual gallantry. It is true that Unit Citations and Commendations by Commanders were awarded but those units were made up of individuals loving and caring for one another and the survival of each other held preeminence. A wounded bomber aircraft is in danger of exploding at any moment. The crewmembers preparing to evacuate, discover one parachute destroyed. A true friend and his disabled and wounded buddy somehow find a way to buckle themselves together, share the same chute, bail out and descend to safety. A damaged bomber, smoke trailing from its engines and falling behind the group formation becomes a "sitting duck" for enemy fighter aircraft. From the formation, a friend in another aircraft sees its plight, drops out of the formation and falls in beside it. Together, they become a more formidable force against an enemy attack. The Master Teacher describes this as follows: ***"Greater love has no one than this, to lay down one's life for his friends." (John 15:13 NIV)***

What should our response be for these surprise accolades? Perhaps this could be an appropriate response. *"My friends and I together cared for one another and our country. Thank you for your recognition."* ✝

How About It?

World War II Veteran's Memorial, on the mall, Washington D.C.

THE PRESENCE

Our C-47 circled the field, then made an approach to the runway somewhere in East Anglia and touched down. As we taxied to the central tarmac area, the airmen of two replacement combat crews looked out on the unfolding scene. Olive drab-colored ambulances with their vivid red crosses painted on the sides and top were lined up facing the field. An assortment of trucks and jeeps sat around in a motley array of positions. The railing along the walkway on the control tower was lined with men, some holding binoculars, scanning the skies.

Scanning the skies, waiting for the returning aircraft

Twenty nervous but excited men exited the plane. We were not the objects of the gathered troops. No one took note of our arrival. Suddenly, the crowd became animated. Everyone's attention was riveted on the sky to the east. Excitement and drama filled the air. The gathering was for the arrival of the returning aircraft and their crews, last seen in the pre-dawn light as they departed for a mission to Germany. Their comrades and friends were coming home. The atmosphere rapidly changed. Aircraft limped in firing green flares. The engines of others had props feathered, smoke and oil trailing out from behind. Jagged holes with conspicuous war damage attested to the reality that they had encountered the enemy. Red flares arching above other returning aircraft set the ambulances in motion, speeding to minister to the wounded, dying and dead aboard.

Aircraft lost over the target did not return. Others were forced to land elsewhere. We were told that fourteen aircraft sustained Class "A" damage, two were considered Class "B". We had not yet learned what that meant. But, we did observe that the morale on base was at a low ebb. Empty bunks in the living quarters, vacant chairs in the mess hall, revetments around the perimeter of the field with no aircraft parked in them were facts, which could not be ignored--- by anyone.

The next morning we met our Squadron Commander Herman Laubrich. He minced no words. He did not gloss over yesterday's mission. "There is a price to pay in conducting a war," he declared. "Yesterday's losses are tragic and unforgettable but we must move on. You are here to replace those who have paid the price with their lives for their country. We do not want you to pay that price. Our purpose in life is to live. If you do not live, you are of no earthly value to your Nation. If you sit out the war in a Prisoner of War camp, all of your training and value as a human being is lost. Both you and your country will suffer. We will do everything we can to help you, but you must cooperate."

Is it unusual for a Commander to show such interest and candor with his troops? Not really. There was a Commander twenty-five hundred years ago who had troops numbered in the thousands…he was also their King. His army listened to him and followed his instructions. This King had a Supreme Commander called God. He was tuned in to God's presence and when he made no move without first consulting God, he did not lose the battle. This was the reason behind his success. He openly confessed his reliance on God and on one occasion addressed his troops with these words, ***"God is our refuge and strength, and always ready to help in times of trouble, so we will not fear." (Psalms 46:1 NLT)*** This Presence worked 2,500 years ago. It worked during those fearful days in World War II and it is still effective in our individual lives today.✝

Coming Home, another mission completed

BE A WINNER

The military vehicles were now parked, the bands had played, the patriotic crowd that had cheered along the parade route now circled the flag pole, and the speakers stand. The color guard and bugler stood by. A light rain began to fall and one-by-one the speakers made their comments. A one-star general spoke. *"Across the decades"*, he declared, *"our young men have bravely fought and have given their lives. Others have survived those war years and are here today as veterans....we honor and recognize you who are among our number today."* He began calling out a list of wars our country had been engaged in during the past six decades. *"How many here today are veterans of World War II?"* The show of hands was few. The Korean War? The Viet Nam War? The Gulf War? He named a number of "peace efforts or policing deployments." There were veterans of each of these wars present!

Surveying the crowd, the General continued, *"Each of these men and women are survivors of these terrible conflicts. We recognize and honor you today. Each of you is a living miracle and has received the mercies and the grace of Almighty God. You could have died, but you did not!"*

I am sure my comrades standing there recalled their own miracles as I did. In my B-24 Liberator bomber while flying high over enemy territory, the flak shell burst between the number two engine and the pilot's compartment. There was no prior warning, it just happened! My left shoulder received the impact of the explosion like a ball bat striking me with full force. The shrapnel ripped open the cockpit, a metal fragment struck the harness of my back pack parachute and penetrated several levels of the webbing and its energy, mostly spent by the time it got to my flesh. Had that fragment struck an inch to the right, I would not have had an arm to hold my Purple Heart medal; had it gone to the left an inch or so, my Purple Heart citation would have been sent to my mother.

Some lived! Some died! Why do such things happen? The answer lies in the fact that you and I are part of life. Life is vulnerable and comes with no guarantees. Time is moving on, we don't have a lot of it to waste. Life will never be perfect living in this world. Every day has some pleasant circumstance, so acknowledge it. There will be pain and hurt every day as well but refuse to bow down or be servants to them. Charles Hadden Spurgeon, a nineteenth century clergyman said, "**The Lord's mercy often rides to the door of our heart upon the black horse of affliction".** The key to peaceful living is to recognize simple things as treasures of great worth. Every moment is a treasure, claim it for God and yourself and you will be a winner! ✟

FACING REALITY

Instinctively, man is always in search of ways to protect himself from the pain of living. Through the ages, regardless of religion, race, or station in life, men have prayed. This seems to be an automatic response to the awareness of danger. Self-preservation is an instinct created in every creature for its own survival. Prayer becomes an enabling element that gives comfort and confidence in overcoming fear. Prayer helps an individual to realize that his help comes from beyond his own created instincts. Instinct alone, breeds fear. Prayer gives mental and spiritual power and strength to deal with and overcome fear, even the fear of death.

Caring for a buddy in need

In 1940, during the height of the Battle of Britain, the Royal Air Force was greatly outnumbered in men and machines. The limited numbers of pilots available for combat were undertrained. Losses were high to German fighter and bomber forces. The Jerrys had combat experienced pilots and unlimited numbers of replacements of aircraft and men. Survival for the British pilots was uncertain. "You didn't spend days moping around," reported one RAF pilot when losses were high and friends were missing or killed. Survivors would remark, "Poor old so–and–so bought it." To play down the gloomy thoughts of death, pilots in some squadrons would place money in a kitty to be kept behind the bar in the club hall so their friends could toast them on the evening of their death. Fear? Certainly! They felt there was little hope for survival.

There was always an increase in the flow of adrenalin when ten American men were assigned to fly a combat mission in a four engine bomber loaded with 2,700 gallons of high octane gasoline and 8,000 pounds of sensitive explosives. Acceleration was sluggish as the machine tediously moved down the 6,000 foot-long runway straining to gain sufficient air speed to become airborne. Once in the air, the anxiety was not over as there were low visibility and the violent turbulence created by the prop wash of aircraft that took off 30 seconds ahead. Once the dozens of aircraft were in combat formation, thoughts of eight hours or more over enemy territory was on everyone's mind. If providence allowed, another mission would be completed, one less mission left to be flown. There was always the question, "Will we complete this one?"

Instinctively, they were filled with uncertainty and fear. Fear is a condition that comes before the possibility of harm, trauma, death, or any unpleasant future event. However, prayer is the ingredient that enables one to be confident in any undertaking because no task is insurmountable. But remember to always be humble before God. No one is invincible. There are no coincidences in God's plan. Everyone is a player in this great divine drama that was written by God, the author and creator of our lives and our destiny. When accompanied by a genuine faith in the Divine, prayer is the most powerful force in the universe. Paul the Apostle declared, *"Always try to do good to each other and to everyone else. Always be joyful, keep on praying. No matter what happens, always be thankful for this is God's will for you who belong to Christ Jesus."* (I Thessalonians 5:16-18 NLT). ✝

GOD LISTENS

During his fighting prime, Muhammad Ali boarded a giant 747 jet headed for his next boxing match. The plane began rumbling toward the runway for takeoff. The flight attendant was routinely checking all passengers to assure that everyone was prepared for the flight. She noticed that Ali had not fastened his seat belt. Looking straight at the brash champ, she requested that he fasten his seat belt. With his characteristic cockiness he snapped, *"Lady, Superman don't need no seat belt!"* Without missing a beat the stewardess responded, *"Superman don't need no plane....so buckle up!"*

People have mentally created the "superman" image and some have even pretended to be one! But such an idea is merely a false illusion. There is no question that each individual in unique....the Psalmist declares....*"I will praise thee; for I am fearfully and wonderfully made: marvelous are thy works." (Psalms 138:14 KJV)*

The generation who attended movies in the 1930's and early 1940's remember the muscular specimen of a man who's prowess was demonstrated as he moved on vines from tree to tree, performing errands of mercy, saving some hapless person in trouble. Now, he is scarcely remembered and/or little known. A recent survey indicated that people age 30 and below had no idea who "Tarzan" was. He was the WWII generation super-person and was followed by "Superman" and now there are others! But all of them will be forgotten as well.

It is too much for the human mind to comprehend the loss of the lives of 50,000,000 human beings during the conflict of World War II. Joseph Stalin, the wartime dictator of the Soviet Union, expressed it well, *"In matters of human perception,"* he is reputed to have said, *"one death constitutes a tragedy, but a million deaths represent only a statistic."* When Stalin lost one of his family members, it was a tragedy...he experienced it and that loss to him was not a mere statistic. This is really the way of life!

Many have deceived themselves by not dealing seriously and directly with their "superman mentality." We are wonderfully complex and we know it! God is always faithful among the millions but He is also faithful on a one-on-one individual encounter. On some unmarked day. . .at some unnoted hour...a God-placed instinct in human hearts becomes alive. When trouble, or loneliness, or lostness is realized, if we respond to God, He will respond to us. God will intervene in your situation. . .at your request. When you call to him, he doesn't turn a deaf ear. He listens! He responds! He acts! *Seek the Lord while He may be found. Call upon Him while he is near. (Isaiah 55:6 NKJ)* ✞

How About It?

An emotional moment

LIFE OR LUCK?

One writer, Frank Murphy, aptly used the gambling term, *"Luck of the Draw"* as an eye arresting title to describe the risky experiences he and thousands of other combat crewmen encountered as they flew missions against Hitler's *Festung Europa,* the so-called European Fortress of the Axis Powers. Judging from the statistics relating to losses and wins, the rate of survival was always in question as the relative security of an English air base was left behind when they flew the cold, hostile skies over Europe. Upon an evaluation of these four words, *"luck of the draw,"* one would assume that the thousands of Americans involved in this game were the players in a giant scheme of survival, those with the *luck,* were the winners. The rest were losers. Sitting around a huge gaming table, the win or lose outcome was decided by the ways in which the cards were dealt.

Is it luck or fate that determines our destiny? The color of your skin, did you have anything to do with it? Your citizenship and nationality, any control over that? What choice did you have in the lineage of your mother and dad or the number of brothers and sisters you have? Did you choose the neighborhood where you spent your childhood, or your father's occupation or profession, or the period of time in history when you lived your life? History has provided a war for just about every generation. As an eligible participant in our war, did you have any choice in where you would fight or the kinds of weapons you would be assigned? What about the military unit and men with whom you would serve and in what battles you would be a participant? Didn't someone else always make that decision? Am I then, just a human robot controlled by the *luck of the draw*?

As a member of the human race, is there anything over which I have control or choice? I might choose to be in good health, have more than enough money, enjoy a loving wife and children, have an honorable and enjoyable profession or occupation, be respected, have a reputation above reproach, and have true-blue lasting friendships. Some or all of these might be life-long goals, but let's face it, not all of them have become reality!

Military fliers are all familiar with contrails, those fluffy white lines of clouds trailing the path of high flying aircraft. When the atmospheric climate is right, the movement of the aircraft through the sky solidifies the cold moist air particles producing highly visible vapors. Aircraft, often obscure because of altitude, can suddenly become visible as contrails begin forming. Just as quickly, the contrails disappear as atmospheric conditions change. The writer of Holy Scripture said, **"For what is your life? It is even a vapor which appears for a little time and then vanishes away." (James 4:14 NKJ)** Our life is just that, a vapor that lasts for a brief period. We are here for a short time and then we are gone.

There are times in our life when the decisions we make have profound and lasting effects on us. These moments of decision are God-given opportunities for us to control and determine our eternal destiny. These are not merely luck or fate. They are God-given allowing you the opportunity to take control of your life. This is not just luck, and it is controlled by your choice.

Will you pray this prayer with me? *Lord, in the midst of a world filled with turmoil, hatred, conflict, unrest, and uncertainty, you give us an opportunity to know you, the Prince of Peace. I cannot in myself change a single thing for which others are responsible, therefore, my inner rest and assurance must come from you. It is not luck but faith and trust in you, that makes me a winner. Thank you for loving me! Amen.* ✝

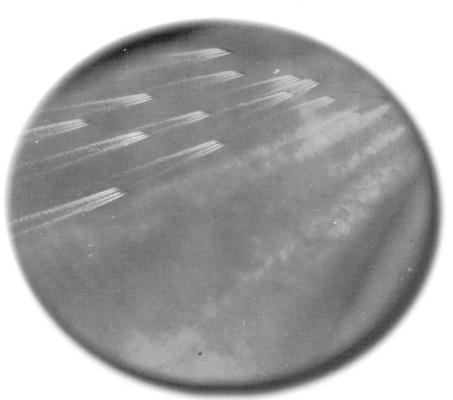

Contrails, like humans, here and soon gone

UNCHANGING THINGS

Of all impressive things, impressive people, impressive organizations, impressive facts, none are permanent. They change, go away and are forgotten. During our time in history, we can remember when many things were very important to us. But, our magnificent achievements don't last long...do they? A contemporary musician sings the lyrics, *"....All of the great kings in the world never endure, all of the great nations in the world never last."* Do you remember Roosevelt, Churchill, Stalin. "Of course you do if you are a WWII veteran. Can you name their aides who helped them on a daily basis? Probably not. But our grandchildren, more than likely, never heard of any of them. Why? Because our magnificent lives and events surrounding them don't last, not even for two generations.

Churchill, no more battles

Just about everything we have learned in science has now changed. Most theories, once proven to be true and workable, are now cast aside because new ones are discovered which are better. Don't discount all of the wonderful things in life that you have been privileged to enjoy. But watch out! These impressive moments of our lives will not last. Have you built your life on that which is enduring?

Kings and kingdoms fall; political systems are unstable and eventually fade away; leaders and their followers are here for awhile and then vanish; wealth flourishes and investors suffer when there is a down-turn in the economy. Almost overnight, science and technology changes. Nothing is permanent. Even our bodies are fading away. Haven't you noticed? We buy eye glasses which help our vision but they do not restore the vision we once had. We place hearing aids in our ears but we still can't hear very well. We take pills to put pep in our step and supplements to stimulate our memory and we must admit that they help for a moment, but they only prolong the inevitable. Now don't knock all of the health fads. We do feel better and our bodies work better, but not on a permanent basis. Everything around us is fading away.

Hearing the church bells strike on the hour was a routine event in the lives of the people of the parish. One night, instead of ringing twice to denote the hour, they kept ringing. They finally stopped at the hundredth ring. The man of the house nudged his wife. *"We'd better get up dear."* he said. *"It's later than it's ever been before!"* And it is! Upon what have we built our future?

It is easy to get caught up in our man-made kingdoms but none of them are permanent. We must change our thinking from the magnificence of this world to the marvels and majesty of God. He is permanent, unchanging, ever loving, compassionate, forgiving and eternal. There is nothing that can compare with Him. And amazing as it is, He loves us. Have you placed your confidence in the eternal love of God? *For God so loved the world that He gave His only begotten Son that whoever believes in Him should not perish but have everlasting life. (John 3:16 NKJ)* ✞

THE PATH

The warriors of 1941-1945 were very concerned and anxious to learn to which theater of war they would be assigned. Once that was determined, appropriate maps were issued and the route to be followed was plotted. The names were strange and there was a lot of blue space denoting the oceans along the route. Looking at the map, the blue areas didn't look very wide but when translated into time for oceanic travel, the hours dragged on. The speed of our aircraft made us question if we would ever see land again. Most of these air-warriors had never seen an ocean before and to be over water, with no land in sight, was an ominous matter.

The bomber crew was made up of students, soda jerks, farmers, mechanics, paper boys, machine operators, taxi drivers, and common part-time laborers. Before our military training, none of us were airmen nor were we specialized in anything. In the nose compartment of our aircraft was our navigator who was just like the rest of us. He was very young and very inexperienced yet he was charting our course. As we had our final briefing before departing the

The Navigator, plotting
his course

continental United States, the officer giving instructions remarked, *"Your destination is England. Don't miss it!"*

Unlike the misguided, misbegotten nineteenth-century army in Paris that set off for the Prussian border without the right maps, we had our maps. A philosopher, A. C. Grayling wrote, *"If you intend a journey, you do well to consult a map."* But it was disconcerting to discover when we were flying over Greenland, this notation was on the map, *"Mountain heights are uncharted."* In other words, you are on your own. Good luck. Don't hit a mountain before you get to England. Someone has remarked about maps, (1) maps lie, (2) no map is accurate, (3) no map is current, (4) no map is impartial, (5) the map will not get you there.

From the time of birth, (a red wrinkled helpless and dependent being) to death (a shriveled, aged, helpless and dependent being), one follows a path of life charted by the situations, choices and opportunities of a lifetime. We pass over uncharted waters and are surrounded by inexperienced fellow travelers like yourself. We come from every walk of life and from every level of society. One's destination is never a place defined in mortal terms but rather a way of looking at things with an eternal perspective.

Using the Bible, our most accurate enduring guide-book, we find a chart and compass for each individual traveler. From Genesis to Revelation there isn't any biblical figure or example that will exactly fit our situation. Each person's map of the world and his life is as peculiar to that individual as a voice print, a thumb-print or DNA. And, we are on our own and our safe arrival depends upon our willingness to follow the Master Chart Maker. A song penned by Edward Hopper in the middle 1800's probably portrays this journey best of all. ✛

Jesus, Savior, pilot me Over life's tempestuous sea.
Unknown waves before me roll, hiding rocks and treach'rous shoal.
Chart and compass **came from Thee; Jesus Savior pilot me.**
When at last I near the shore, and the fearful breakers roar...
May I hear thee say to me, "Fear not, I will pilot thee."

GOOD GAME

Peppermint Patty, the more athletic than scholarly tomboy, created by Charles Schulz, is the subject of one of his final cartoon strips. For over fifty years Schulz created the "Peanuts" cartoon comedy featuring Charlie Brown, Lucy, Linus, Marcie, Schroeder, Pig Pen, the bird Woodstock, the dog Snoopy and several other colorful and lovable characters. Across fifty years, these interesting little guys have appeared in four feature films, are the theme of three amusement parks and books numbering over 300 million copies. Because of failing health, Schulz is calling it quits. Every message is always funny, thought provoking, philosophical. He has attracted readers young and old. His lessons imbues "Peanuts" with gentle lessons in faith, hope, and charity.

Football on British soil, win or lose, it was fun

What was his parting lesson to us? Peppermint Patty is on a football field, talking as usual, to an unseen individual. She is in a crawling position on a rain-drenched playing field. She is pictured in both up and down stances in the mud calling the plays and giving instructions, *"Its your ball," "fourth down." "Chuck, are you gonna run or pass?"* Appearing from behind, Marcie shows up carrying a yellow umbrella stating: *"Everyone's gone home sir," "you should go home too it's getting dark."* Peppermint Patty remarks *"We had fun, didn't we Marcie?"* Turning back from where she came, sloshing in the puddles, and peering into the foggy darkness, Marcia replies, *"Yes sir, we had fun."* Shultz, in his parting words to millions sums it up with Peppermint Patty exclaiming, *"Nobody shook hands and said 'good game.'"*

Hopefully, life doesn't end like that for us with only a few fans around. But in many cases, it does. Our acquaintances are as diverse as the characters in "Peanuts". Our experiences have plots which develop, often unpleasantly and not to our liking. The things in life that only happen to the other fellow, actually happen to us. In our innocent behavior, we are often knocked flat because we are misunderstood. Friendships often turn sour because those we trusted prove to be selfish and self-serving people. Unexpectedly our health fails or our portfolio of financial security is affected by outside forces over which we have no control. Like Peppermint Patty, we may feel like *"Nobody shook hands and said, 'Good Game.'"*

Although this may happen, we are not going to sit on the sidelines because we are unwilling to take a risk. Experience has taught that it pays to live by the Golden Rule**. . ."Therefore, whatever you want men to do to you, do also to them" (Matthew 7:12 NKJ)** While sloshing through life, we may wonder how did we make it through this or that experience? But we always do and in the midst of living our life whether or not we receive the encouraging "high fives", we shall hang on. Our own inner strength and self-esteem berthed from doing what is right will keep us going. **"Do unto others"** by giving them the same encouragement you would desire. Life is too short to do otherwise. ✝

COMFORTING WORDS

The first outing of a fledgling recruit on a military base at night presented a frightening and unexpected experience. While he stumbled along in the dark on an unfamiliar street, an authoritative and threatening command pierced the chilly night air. "HALT, WHO GOES THERE?" There was no question as to what to do. . . stop in your tracks, and do it now! The second command followed immediately, "ADVANCE AND BE RECOGNIZED". Name, rank, serial number, unit assignment, jingling dog tags, the proper uniform seemed to satisfy the shadowy figure who posed the questions. The order, "PROCEED", brought relief.

Proper credentials are always in order. Everyone faces the questions, *"Who am I?" "What am I doing here?"* and *"where am I going?"* These questions almost always come during moments of crises. Wartime encounters are prime examples. In wars throughout history, soldiers on opposing sides have relied heavily on their Creator for comfort. German soldiers in the past wore buckles with the inscription ***"Gott mit uns"*** (God is with us). Russian soldiers, it is said, also had buckles with the inscription ***"Bog s nami"*** (God is with us). The English and Belgians had the motto ***"Dieu et mon Droit"*** (God and my right): the Americans ***"God and my country"***. Every nation wants to have God and right on its side. How can this be? All have different languages, political agendas, uniforms, methods of killing. In short, there is little resemblance of being alike. But, we all want God.

A squadron commander of B-17's speaking after a coordinated FW-190 fighter plane attack slashed through his formations knocking down a great number of Flying Forts mourned, *"I lost sixty men in a single day."* He went on to say, *"It didn't fill me with hatred against the enemy. I have never liked the Germans but they were doing their job just as we were."*

God is saying, regardless of our political affiliation, "Advance and be recognized". Name, rank, serial numbers, nationality, are not enough. Hundreds of wars and passing decades only prove that goodness and righteousness cannot be legislated and enforced by a gun or a political ideology. Goodness cannot be imposed externally from the top down; it must grow internally. The Nazi dictator and self-proclaimed Master Manipulator of all ages used his selfish power to coerce, to dazzle and to force his ideology upon all humankind regardless of their creed, nationality or color. God's persuasion, on the other hand, is non-coercive. It knows no national boundaries. What makes us human is not our political leanings, it is not our mind, but our heart. It is not our ability to persuade but rather our ability to love.

It is a matter of personal choice. One declared, **"Choose this day whom you will serve. . . as for me and my house, we will serve the Lord." (Joshua 24:15 KJV)** Whom have you chosen? ✝

How About It?

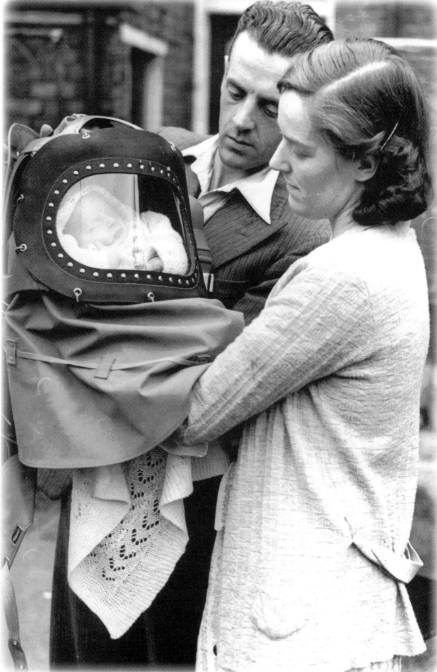

Caring British parents protecting their infant with a gas mask device

How About It?

THE BET AT BARTH

In wartime, a place called Barth was Hell. It was a prisoner of war camp located only a few miles south of the Baltic Sea in Northern Germany. Downed aircrews were interned there after having been shot down and captured by the enemy. Ten thousand were held there as prisoners. The camp was divided into four administrative compounds with 2,500 airman in each unit. These "guests of the Germans" were elite and quality men -- leaders and brave American youth. They had been effective in their aerial combat activity against Nazi Germany. But now, their role had dramatically changed.

Internment brought suffering beyond belief; the unending frigid weather, crowded uncomfortable quarters; the unpredictable behavior of the guards; inadequate food, lice, sickness, boredom, death by starvation or by exposure was their unchanging agenda. Yet, there were times when the spirits of the POW'S were lifted. It was always through their own methods of creativity and ingenious that this happened. One on-going "high" was when each new contingent of "guests" arrived in camp. Up-to-date uncensored information became immediately available. The reports brought in by these new POW'S gave fresh, unbiased running accounts of how the war was progressing on the Eastern Front with the Russians and the Western Front as well. The increasing numbers of bombers and fighters appearing in the air overhead brought silent but joyful hope to Barth's imprisoned.

As optimism flourished, small group conversations centered on the war's end and their freedom. Liberation was on everyone's lips. Talk of being home for Christmas became a Utopian Dream. Although all embraced the Dream, not all were optimistic. This difference in opinion brought about the "Bet at Barth" A wager was on. New life came to the camp. But what was there to wager? There was no money, no freedom or 3-day passes, no material possessions for the loser to forfeit, no points or promotions to be gained or lost. In a heated conversation, two men got carried away in their claims. An optimistic airman bet a pessimistic one on the following terms. "If we aren't home by Christmas, I will kiss your ass before the whole group formation right after head-count on Christmas morning." They shook hands. The bet was on! Well, the optimist hadn't counted on the Battle of the Bulge in early December. Consequently, the war was prolonged and they were still in Barth on Christmas Day, 1944.

Christmas morning was cold, there was snow on the ground and frigid air was blowing in off the Baltic Sea. The body count for the compound began, each man was counted off, *ein, zwei, drei, vier, funf, sechs, sieben, acht*. Under ordinary circumstances, when the counting was completed and the German Guards were satisfied that everyone was accounted for, the group split up and everyone went to his barracks. But this time, everybody stayed in formation. The two betting "Kriegies" walked out of the formation and went into the barracks. No one else moved! The guards were puzzled. They didn't know what was going on. Soon, the two men came out of the barracks. One was carrying a bucket of water with a towel folded over his other arm. The second one marched to the front of the formation, turned his back toward the assembled troops and guards, pulled down his pants and stooped over. The other took the towel, dipped it in the soapy water and washed the exposed posterior. The whole formation was standing there looking and laughing. The German guards and dignitaries of Barth stood gazing in amazement. Then the optimist bent over and kissed his opponent on the rear! A mighty cheer went up from over 2,000 men. Then the puzzled guards joined in on the fun.

Nothing changed on Christmas Day, just the same black bread and thin soup, sparse and flavorless. As evening fell, the weather worsened, the barracks were cold, the last of the daily allotted coal briquettes were reduced to nothing but white ash. Boredom was settling in and they anticipated another long miserable night. Suddenly, the door opened. . .a voice shouted, "The curfew has been lifted for tonight! We're going to have a Christmas service over in the next compound." The weather was bitterly cold, the new fallen snow crunched under the feet of the men as they quickly shuffled towards their congregating comrades in the distance.

Nazi prisoner of war camp

The nightly curfew always kept the men inside . . . this Christmas night's reprieve allowed them to be outside after dark for the first time. Above, the stars were shining brightly and high in the northern skies, the dim flicker of Aurora Borealis added a magical touch as the troops assembled. Gratitude was felt in their hearts. . .a lone singer led out with one of the world's most loved and known carols. Others joined in and soon there was joyful worship ringing throughout the camp.

> Silent night! Holy night!
> All is calm, all is bright.

The German guards marching their beats stopped in their tracks. . .they turned their heads toward the music. The words were unfamiliar but they recognized the tune. . .after all, ***Stille Nacht, Heilige Nacht*** was composed by a German. They loosened up, smiled, and joined in the celebration...the praise became bilingual.

Round yon virgin mother and Child
Cinsam wacht nurdas traute hoch heilige Paar

Holy Infant, so tender and mild
Holder Knabe im lockigen Hoiar

Sleep in heavenly peace, sleep in heavenly peace.
Schlaf in himmlischer ruh', schlaf in himmlischer ruh'.

The Bet at Barth had paid off. Everyone had won! As the words of the carol rang in their hearts, there was a literal fulfillment. Tonight they would sleep in peace. War and internment did not have the power to destroy the meaning and beauty of this special day.

It was Christmas. They were not at home. But they declared, "Next year we will be! All of us!" And they were! ✞

PURPOSE IN LIFE?

The wall in a maternity ward has an inscription which reads, "A baby is God's opinion that the world should go on." In the first three decades of this century, God was sending a strong message to freedom-loving people everywhere that he had a specific purpose for every baby born during this time in history. These babies were nurtured by God-fearing parents and a society which expected integrity, industry, and patriotism. As they grew into their teen years, the war clouds of oppression arose to destroy the ideals which they had been taught to respect. Challenged, they responded to the call of their country. They went into an atmosphere of regimentation preparing them for duty and often, the supreme sacrifice. Still they went... by the thousands and then by the millions. They went from tranquility and confidence to an atmosphere of violence and fear.

Jewish victims of Nazi brutality

What happened did not seem fair. Some were single and survived. Others didn't live to see their new baby. Some were maimed for life and others came through unscathed. Some lie in hallowed resting places in England, Brittany, Lorraine and the Ardennes, yet many came home to live lives of comfort, achievement and happiness. The lives and talents of many were destroyed, others were able to use theirs to enable people around the world to enjoy freedom purchased at such a high cost. There is no simple explanation. All of us are pressing through life, some press longer than others. Many reach the promised three-score and ten. Others do not.

How could these wasted talents have been put to use had they not been destroyed? We do not know, of course. But we, as a part of the legacy that has been spared, must recognize that Divine intervention allowed us to survive. How have we used and how are we now using our gifts and talents? Are we tiptoeing through each day, week, and year just so we can reach death safely? We should be praying, "Lord, wake me up before I die." Life can get away! Don't be satisfied with just breathing God's free air. Pump blood, but pump it with a purpose.

Your law is my delight. Let my soul live, and it shall praise you. And let Your judgments help me. (Psalms 119:17-18) ✝

Dachau, Nazi Concentration Camp. Over 206,000 prisoners (mostly Jewish) were known to have endured indescribable suffering and death at this place

Post War memorial for those who died at Dachau 1933-1945

Eating and drinking, Oshkosh, Wisconsin

Celebrating with the Brits

How About It?

ABOUT TIME

We have heard it said that "Time waits for no man", and as the supply of time dwindles in a person's life, one suddenly realizes that if you don't use what Mother Nature gave you, Father Time will take it and there is no getting it back.

The element called "time" has always been important in man's scheme of things. Pony Express riders in pioneer days mounted their steeds and dashed furiously across the prairie, changed to fresh horses frequently, and on and on they tirelessly rode to deliver their precious mail pouch. All of this was done in the interest of time. The automobile came along with the speed of a mile-a-minute and that was really moving. Then the airplane helped mankind to go even faster. Society and the military establishment constantly demanded more and more speed. When a test pilot broke the sound barrier, he became a national icon. Now we discuss speeds in terms of Mach 1, Mach 2 and Mach 3, speeds that are not uncommon these days. Space travel has given us a new dimension of time. A rocket fired into the atmosphere can get across oceans and continents before an ocean-going vessel can get away from its dock.

Time is of essence in ironing out the "bugs" of our computer-driven society. As society enters the twenty-first century, we have heard the term "Y2K" over and over. We have been instructed to get our computers in compliance with the changes that would be coming. How wonderful it is to have lived through a part of the twentieth century and the old millennium and be moving into the twenty-first century and a new millennium with its many challenges. It's hard to imagine what lies ahead!

The song writer penned these words. . ."*Yesterday is gone, tomorrow may never come. . .but we have this moment.*" This moment of time is ours. With our mortality so certain and our destiny so dependent upon the mercies of God, we can't afford to waste time and neglect getting our Spirit in compliance with out Creator. Solomon, recognized as the wisest man on earth, talked about time: "***There is a time for everything, a season for every activity under heaven. A time to be born and a time to die.***" He goes ahead to list a number of timely events spread throughout life but he summarizes it all when he declared, "***There is nothing better for people than to be happy and to enjoy themselves as long as they can. And people should eat and drink and enjoy the fruits of the labor, for these are the gifts of God." (Ecclesiastes 3:12-13 NLT)***

Time is our most precious commodity. Use it or lose it forever! ✝

MOMENT OF TRUTH

Two adolescent youngsters decided to try an experiment to determine how dedicated and truthful the parishioners in the local rural church really were. The pastor was preaching to a fullhouse. Every pew was occupied and the congregation was listening intently to every word he spoke. Behind the scenes, one of the tricksters put on his costume and at a key moment, stepped onto the platform in full view of everyone. To say the least, the red garb complete with horns, pitchfork, long tail with a pointed end, and mean-looking mask got everyone's attention. Without the spook saying a word, the entire congregation, including the pastor, made a wild dash for the exit in the rear. In the melee, a handicapped

grandma was left sitting near the front, all alone. Unable to move, she sat there shaking and wondering about her fate. The red-garbed creature crept up to her. His fierce look didn't add to her comfort. Trembling, she broke the silence..."Old Devil", she squeaked out, *"I, I, I, I, haaaasa been a,a,a, on your side all along!*

It used to be that a man's simple act of offering a handshake was his bond. What he said, he meant. It was accepted! Now, we seem to be getting away from that. Not everyone has fallen prey to this compromise but it appears that regardless of station in life or position, high or low, a statement taken under oath doesn't mean what it used to. We haven't been guilty, or have we?

Recently, I ran across a testimony given by a navigator in one of the Eighth Air Force Bomb Groups who was flying missions out of England against Germany. The attrition rate was high and survival, at best, seemed elusive. This very truthful airman said, *"When things got sticky on a mission, I would probably say to God that if he would get me through this one, I'd be a good boy and go to temple. I'd try anything at such times, but I never meant to go through with them, and never did."* This man lived and filled a successful career. He wrote this testimony. . .I wonder what has he done about that youthful pledge since he has grown older?

No doubt, we have all felt terribly hopeless at times. We have made promises, often very sincere promises, and failed miserably in our vows. Have we "been on the Devil's side all along?" Or, do we encounter him face-to-face with courage? God is saying to us, "I love you, I love you, I love you". Then God asks, "Will the road you're on get you to my Place?"

"Don't ever swear for you can't turn one hair white or black. Say just a simple 'Yes I will' or 'No, I won't.' Your word is enough. To strengthen your promise with a vow shows that something is wrong." (Matt.5:36-37 NLT) ✝

A moment of truth, Memorial Service, George Lymburn, Madingley Cemetery, 1995

CHOICES

Life is not made up of a few big events but of countless smaller happenings consuming millions of minute lapses of time. These time bytes allotted to us by our Creator are often expended thoughtlessly. Expressions such as: "just a second," "one moment please," "wait here," "not so fast," "hold it," are examples. These waiting patterns imposed upon us by society and ourselves can consume much of our life. Every time byte expended is gone forever, but the resulting behavior or response may be with us all of our days.

Courtship between a young man and woman requires effort and time but when they stand side-by-side in a marriage ceremony and make a vow, both declare to love and cherish "unto death do us part." They commit themselves to endless encounters with sorrow or joy, frustration or satisfaction, poverty or riches, sickness or health. All are included in the marriage contract. Relationships are important and time invested in this way is not lost.

A profound commitment

A fledgling civilian, when requested to serve his country and Uncle Sam, raises his right hand before a designated authority and he swears." **I will** bear true faith and allegiance to the United States of America; **I will** serve them honestly and faithfully against all enemies whomsoever; and that **I will** obey the President of the United States, and the orders of the officers appointed over me according to the Rules and Articles of the government of the United States." With three "I wills" and a little over 50 additional words, he puts his life "in hock" for the duration.

Every task, regardless of its simplicity, requires countless decisions, each of which uses precious time. How easy it is also to allow others to use up our life with no real goals achieved. We must be ready, when the moment comes, to use our time wisely. Often, time wasting bytes slip up on us, and opportunities lost may determine our destiny as well as the destiny of others. Henry David Thoreau has expressed it. . ."*As if you could kill time without injuring eternity.*" ✞

IN PURSUIT

Americans look to one of the most time-honored statements in the Declaration of Independence as the ultimate in personal freedom and privilege. The phrase, **Life, liberty, and the pursuit of happiness** cited in this document is the marvelous aspiration of humankind everywhere. If you are reading this page, you have **life** and are enjoying the first part of this declaration. We benefit, on a daily basis, the privileges and blessings of **liberty**, the second part of this statement. But, **the pursuit of happiness** is something that is not automatic.

Folks spend a lot of time, money, and effort chasing after happiness. The things we do to seek happiness are often pretty shallow and empty the next morning. Consider this: maybe happiness is pursuing us but it never catches up.

Solomon, a very wise man said, **"But happy is he that keeps the law."** **(Proverbs 29:18 NKJ)** God created both physical and spiritual laws and a person in **pursuit of happiness** must be in harmony with those laws. It must be remembered that happiness is not your reward, it is a consequence. If happiness is going to become a part of you, get rid of selfishness and dishonesty, anger and guilt, and all other roadblocks that keep it from catching up. Clear out these obstacles, keep them out of your life, and happiness will surprise you by moving up close, and it will be a wonderful traveling companion. And as you travel along, remember, happiness is not your destination, it is your lifestyle.

The pursuit of happiness... is it catching up with you or is it falling behind? Check on your progress in this quest. The overtures to happiness are: (1) something to do, (2) something to love, and (3) something to hope for. If you are falling behind, then pray, "*Lord, please give me enough sense to see that happiness only comes when I follow the route you have chosen for me.*" If happiness is your companion, praise Him for his faithfulness. In another place in scripture, Solomon declares: **"Happy is the man who finds wisdom. And the man who gains understanding." (Proverbs 3:13 NKJ)** ✝

How About It?

For I dipt into the future, far as human eye could see,
Saw the Vision of the world, and all the wonder that would be:
Saw the heavens fill with commerce, argosies of magic sails,
Pilots of the purple twilight, dropping down with costly bales.
Heard the heavens fill with shouting, and there rained a ghastly dew
From the nations airy navies grappling in the central blue.

Far along the world-wide whisper of the south-wind rushing warm
With the standards of the peoples, plunging, through the
thunderstorm;
Till the war-drum throbbed no longer, and the battle-flags were
furled
In the parliament of man, the Federation of the World.

from
Locksley Hall
by Lord Alfred Tennyson
published 1842, 100 years before World War II

GOD'S TIMING

Death, there's only one per customer, so it must be a real bargain! The trouble is, we just don't know when we can cash in on it.

A fact that just about everyone considers at one time or another is that there are no guarantees regarding the length of life. Now, King David of the Bible does mention a time-line, ***"The days of our life are seventy years, And if by reason or strength they are eighty years....for it is soon cut off and we fly away." (Psalms 90:10 NKJ)*** Obituaries are listed in alphabetical order but not in chronological order. The young and the very old are right there on the page side-by-side.

Crosses and Stars of David, dust and wind in the air

I have observed veterans in reunion, still wondering about the timing of the deaths of their friends while they were spared. At military cemeteries standing among all of the Crosses and Stars of David markers, eyes are moist and emotions are high when a Memorial Service is conducted. In life, a young person has a particular illness and dies while a much older person whose life is almost spent survives from the same illness. The age-old question arises, "Why does this happen?" Many address the Almighty, "Why me Lord?" These are tough questions to answer, yet a few feeble words of explanation might be helpful.

Whether we die young or old, our years on earth are nothing in comparison to eternity. In the lyrics of the rock and roll song "Kansas" we are spoken of as "dust and wind in the air", all we are is dust. While our dust blows in the wind, we must make the moments count. Do we have so many items on our agenda that count for nothing? Does our dust in the air make people wonder who we really are? We ought to be amazing people, touching others with enough genuine love to make our "dust" count. Someone has said the art of aging is to become more accepting and more grateful. *"The incredible calculus of old age is: as more is taken, there is more love for what remains."* The wise Psalmist continues ***"So teach us to number our days, That we may gain a heart of wisdom. . .that we may rejoice and be glad ALL of our days." (Psalms 90:12,14a NKJ)*** ✝

COOPERATION

St. Peter approached a brave but undecorated airman and asked him if he could be granted one wish, what would it be? The unassuming airman was totally amazed but after careful thought he said he would like to spend a brief time in Hell, an equal time in Heaven, and then return to earth to live out his life. With this unusual request, St. Peter went for the Father's approval. "Granted," He responded.

Team effort, the secret of success

First was Hell. Large banquet tables were loaded with food of every description. But, those seated at the table were sad, glum, grumbling, unhappy. They were sallow-faced, gaunt, starving people. The young airman couldn't believe his eyes. "With all of these wonderful foods, why are they so unhappy and starving?" Then he noticed. Both arms on every individual had a restrainer that kept them from bending their elbows. They could not lift the food to their mouths. As delectable as the food appeared, it was of no value. They were starving.

Then he visited Heaven. The very same scene was present, except that those seated around the banquet table were happy and well fed and the whole atmosphere was jovial. The guests had the same kind of restrainers on their arms as the folks in Hell. The difference? Although they could not flex their arms and feed themselves, they were joyfully feeding and serving each other. The restrainers posed problems but through cooperation, they were living an abundant life.

In war, airmen survived through cooperation. It was a team effort. There were pre-mission photo reconnaissance flights into enemy territory to gather weather and target information; intelligence units interpreted and commanders made decisions on that information; ground personnel prepared and loaded the aircraft and briefing personnel forecasted what to expect on the mission; air crews manned the aircraft; scout pilots went ahead to direct the bomber formations through the weather; fighter pilots gave air cover; crewmen administered emergency in-flight first aid to the wounded; and ground controllers guided crippled aircraft safely home. Everyone worked together.

Cooperation is the difference between Heaven and Hell. This was learned in the crucible of war. It works in peacetime as well. The Father tells us how. **"Be kind to each other, tender hearted, forgiving one another, just as God has forgiven you because you belong to Christ." (Ephesians 4:32 NLT)** ✝

RIDING IN THE BACK

Curled and wadded up in their turrets or standing at the waist window for hours with an arctic wind blasting away at them, gunners on a heavy bomber were indispensable. Without caution, frost bite was almost certain. As their aircraft jostled for position in the formation, as the drone of the engines changed, as violent maneuvers occurred unexpectedly, the constant swaying of the aircraft always left them wondering what was going on up front. Were these sudden changes normal or was disaster just waiting to happen?

The early concept of having gunners on bomber aircraft was defensive in nature. Bombers were envisioned as "fortresses" bristling with rapid-fire guns pointing in every direction to discourage and deter enemy fighter attack. This idea worked. In addition to bombs being painted on the aircraft indicating missions flown, swastikas were added indicating the number of "enemy kills" which could be attributed to the skills of the gunners. The number of bombers "saved" as a result of these airmen can never be documented. We would be amazed if we knew. The gunners were also the so-called "eyes in the back of the head of the pilot". Without their visual reports, the up-front crewmen didn't and couldn't know what was happening in the airspace to the rear. They relayed the status of the formation squadrons, groups, and divisions as the dozens of aircraft moved into place forming the bomber stream for the mission.

They were always alert, watching the engines for tell-tale signs of smoke or fire, oil and fuel leaks, or damage to the aircraft. They watched out for each other's safety. Their eyes scanned blinding white skies for enemy aircraft and when an attack was certain, only then did they break intercom silence. They watched as black bursts of flak followed them along in the sky and flinched as the "crump, crump, crump" of bursting shells and the odor of cordite filled their compartments. They watched as holes appeared in their aircraft and when a buddy was wounded, they became Florence Nightingales, nurses of the air. Their assignment was demanding and very lonely. How did they stand up to the pressure?

Somewhere in their upbringing, these airmen learned courage and obedience. Their early military discipline of mastering without question three basic statements, ie., "Yes sir, No sir, and No excuse sir" were tools which strengthened their determination to survive. A war-time commander summed it up best in five words, *"Training and discipline pays off."* The wonderful thing about gunners is that they were **human.** They lost their tempers and became angry, they got cold and hungry, scolded God, were egotistical or testy, impatient, made mistakes and regretted them, admitted their fear and didn't try to hide it. Still they went on doggedly blundering toward heaven. Their attitude seemed to be *". . . when you have done all those things which you are commanded say, 'We have done what was our duty to do'" (Luke 17:19 NKJ)* These airmen, these gunners, were giants of courage and fortitude, honored by their pilots and their comrades. ♱

A gunner on the job

TAP INTO YOUR MEMORIES

It is incredible how much alike we humans are in appearance...well hardly. Personality, never! Achievements, non! But under all of these characteristics, the real person shares almost every emotion, desire, and thought. Thought, you say? Well, thought patterns do seem to center around three basic concepts.

Aging "Warriors" gathering at a military convention have received invitations from their leadership to attend a well planned program of activities. Reservations are made, money is sent, travel plans are finalized. Chats on the phone with their buddies about attending preceed the actual day of arrival. Wartime friends show up, individual gatherings are inevitable, conversations are lively and spirited, and stories are shared, generally with some exaggeration. After 25 years of repetition, the stories are perfected and almost believable. In this group, there may be a sprinkling of Generals or Corporals and lots of rank in between, and all are thinking of the past, the present, and/or the future. . .there is nothing else. These are the three ingredients that make up the fabric of everyone's life. All thoughts center around them.

Memories of the past are certainly resurrected when wartime experiences are recalled. Many experiences were not pleasant but their shared memories are allies to uplift one another. Memories, dreams and today's realities, even the bad times, can hold some good to those who refuse to succumb to defeat. Memories of failure awaken the fear of failing again while memories of success build confidence required to achieve further success. In memory, we recall times of terror, boredom, suffering, peace, comfort, thrills, excitement and victories. Strength and a greater sensitivity towards events happening in the present are the rewards of those who refuse to be defeated. Today's events are tomorrow's memories that bring pleasant anticipation for the future. So, the three thought patterns we all share are memories of the past, our present activities, and thoughts of the future. The power of memories is only a heartbeat away. Tap into your memories and bring a sense of wonder back into your life.

"I have considered the days of old. I call to remembrance my song in the night. I meditate within my heart. And my spirit makes diligent search." (Psalms 77:5-6 NKJ)

"The memory of the just is blessed." (Proverbs 10:7a NKJ) ✝

A U.S.O. Saturday night dance

In remembrance, Bill and Norma Beasley

THE MYSTIC BOND

There weren't a lot of exciting activities to while-away the time on an American airbase in wartime England during World War II. Living quarters fell short of having a four star rating. Two rows of twelve single iron beds, (twenty-four in all) with square "biscuits" of hard padding serving as mattresses, the high vaulted ceiling with open rafters and roofing nails showing through, the bare concrete slab floor and the single pot-bellied stove in the middle of the room; this was the airmen's home away from home. But home it was! There were hours, days and weeks of endless boredom shattered with moments of total terror when in combat. We had in common certain traits: we were Americans, we had a common foe, we had a goal of getting out of this conflict alive, and we had genuine compassion and concern for the safety of each other.

Buddies 'at ease'

Our lives were somewhat structured. When not flying combat missions, we practiced instrument flying in the Link trainer, participated in gunnery practice and formation flying. We attended briefing sessions given by the Operations Officer or heard lectures on Escape and Evasion by those who had made their way home from behind enemy lines.

Everyone regardless of rank or status felt boredom. Fatigue was ever present, sometimes real and sometimes brought on by sheer frustration. To cope, everyone participated throughout the day in "sack-time," relaxing and sleeping with their clothes on in their "luxurious" living quarters, oblivious to the din going on at the other twenty-three beds. Some would have just returned from mail call, others using their knee as a writing table wrote letters or updated their diaries. Others watched as a "care package" was opened,. hoping for something that might be shared. Card games were constantly in progress and someone always stoked the fire in the highly inefficient heating stove. A trip to the Post Exchange brought commodities into the barracks that were bartered among interested individuals; candy for tobacco, or chewing gum for soap. Everyone always came away a winner.

There was also the Post Theater that we called the Opera House. It was not an imposing place, only a Quonset hut with a projector in one end and a large sheet at the other with about a hundred metal chairs lined up in irregular rows. Even a slight movement by the occupants created a scraping din on the concrete floor. This did not help in understanding the scratchy sound track of the film. Top of the line Hollywood productions were always on the docket, preceded by our favorite feature, a current Paramount News Reel. The viewers were anxious to see these and get the latest scoop on the war effort around the world. What was going on in North Africa, the Russian front, in the Pacific War, on the home front? Whenever there was good news there was cheering. But one scene dampened the enthusiasm of the crowd. A beautiful flight of 8th Air Force bombers was gliding along in perfect formation toward enemy territory. A close-up shot presented a scene with which we were all very familiar. A direct flack hit on the left wing slung the plane into a spiral of flame. There were no parachutes. All were lost. As a result of this scene, the flight crewmembers arose from their seats and exited the building.

Camaraderie

Those not attending the movie understood perfectly the fear, anger, and anxiety of their comrades when they returned to their barracks and related what had happened. All had made the trek through the "valley of the shadow of death" more than once. We had made the journey safely, but others had not. If one made it through one day, he might not another. The newsreel showed one crew that did not make it. The loss to those who viewed the film was as real as if one of our own crews had gone down.

The camaraderie demonstrated that night in the barracks exists even now wherever the warriors of the Mighty Eighth Air Force get together. Some cannot understand the bond we share when our time together was so short. Perhaps we cannot understand it ourselves. But it is very real. Although our civilian lives have lead us in many directions, as we grow older, this mystic bond still exists and grows stronger, into a bond that cannot be explained or broken. ✝

CATCHING UP!

I have been to lots of meetings involving Eighth Air Force men and women. I have looked them over and have had many opportunities to hear their stories and learn a lot about them. But I have never heard of a single one of them who became important enough to have his portrait on a postage stamp or have a street or a building named after him or have a day set aside by Congress when all federal employees and schools get a day off. And probably, the flag will never be flown at half-mast for any of us.

But what a great bunch of fellows! We survived a war and came home to a nation that geared up for our return. We veterans were enabled to get an education because of the G.I. Bill. Weddings became big business. Marriage and family were celebrated. We constructed homes and filled them with furniture and appliances. In our generation television, the interstate highway system, suburbia, space travel, satellites, computers and new methods in medical technology have all been developed and invented. The beautiful thing about it is that we helped make all of this happen. Then, while all of this was occurring, we produced the baby boomers and educated them, helped them to fit into society and develop a work ethic that produced a work force that made our nation the greatest. Now all of that is history.

Our gray hairs, are growing out of our ears instead of our heads. What next? I received a letter from an old buddy in our outfit who was looking forward to attending the next big reunion if "the good Lord is willing and the creeks don't rise." He declared that he was feeling his age (he is 86). He has the care of an invalid wife that gets a little "wearying" sometimes. He adds, "but, I spent too much time preparing myself for this life and not enough for the next one, so, I 'gotta' catch up."

In this regard, may God bless us all! ☦

They gave everything

Catching up

BIRTHDAYS, HOW MANY?

Birthdays are something that everyone has in common. Birthdays. Some of us have more of them than others but every year that rolls around, we add another one. Someone once said that the secret of staying young is to live honestly, eat slowly, and lie about your age. But having many years under your belt isn't all that bad. Now, I believe in staying young (in spirit) without lying about it. Aging is a process we can't avoid (there is another alternative to growing old but what sane person seeks it). Each birthday enriches our lives and we are one year the wiser. Older? We joke about it, we groan about our pains, we resist it but we can't stop it! We have questions about what happens when we stop having these annual events in our

Jimmy Stewart, B-24 pilot

lives. What happens when we are no longer around to celebrate? Is death when we go to sleep or is death when we finally wake up?

In the middle of May, a group of B-24 fellows were together and it was mentioned that Jimmy Stewart was going to have his 89th birthday. Someone had a card and all of us signed it and sent it off to him. He got the card and looked over the names. Some of the guys he knew from back in WWII days with the 8th Air Force. Others in their 75+ years of hardly legible penmanship signatures baffled him but he received our greetings with his customary grace. A short time later, he experienced what we were discussing earlier - death.

The number invited to his funeral was small. The service was simple with the pastor, James Morrison reading several passages from the Bible. Then Jimmy's daughter, Kelly, spoke briefly and movingly about her dad, concluding, *"Here's to our father, the richest man in town"*. The reference was, of course, from **"It's a Wonderful Life"**. The service ended with Taps being played and then Auld Lang Syne was sung. A very moving tribute for a great American, a screen star, a devoted husband and father, a compassionate military commander, a skilled B-24 pilot and a gentleman.

So, what do we do with birthdays? Don't try to avoid them because you can't! Don't be surprised when the candles cost more than the cake. Just as General Jimmy Stewart was not exempt from the grave, neither are we. Don't try to avoid your birthdays, welcome them as mile-markers that are reminders that you aren't home yet, your tour of duty is not finished, but you're closer than you've ever been. *"Yea, though I walk through the valley of the shadow of death, I will fear no evil; for You are with me; Your rod and Your staff, they comfort me." (Psalms 23:4 NKJ)* ☩

> *"We have questions about what happens*
> *when we stop having birthdays,*
> *those annual events in our lives.*
> *What happens when we are*
> *no longer around to celebrate?*
> *Is death when we go to sleep or is death*
> *when we finally wake up?"*

How About It?

MORE THAN BOLDNESS

Between 1939 and 1941, The Air Staff of the U.S. Army began organizing for war. On June 20, 1941, the Army Air Corps became the Army Air Force. War raged in Europe and in the Pacific. The war in Europe was given priority and the military leadership in Washington, D.C. felt that a total of 239 air groups and more than two million men in the air arm would be necessary to gain victory over the Axis. Their projection was to produce 60,000 aircraft annually. At the time when these goals were set, the Air Corps had fewer than 2,000 flying officers and less than 1,000 aircraft.

A vigorous recruitment and training program for airmen was undertaken. New weapons of war were designed; to build these weapons, factories were springing up everywhere. Civilians who had little or no industrial experience migrated to the work place to produce them. Military bases were established all over the country. Munitions, equipment, supplies, service and transportation, had to be provided. Mobilization activity was seen everywhere and America's patriotism and loyalty reached an all-time high. A fighting force rapidly emerged. The VIII Bomber Command and the VIII Fighter Command were formed. Military leaders were sent to England, sites for air bases were identified and facilities had to be built. Plans were formulated, supply for these forces had to be anticipated, men and machines were to be deployed. Then on August 17, 1942, twelve B-17 Flying Fortresses undertook the first Eighth Air Force bombing mission. The Marshalling yards at Rouen, France was the first target.

From August, 1942 until May, 1945 the Eighth Air Force grew in strength and pounded targets throughout the continent of Europe until the resources and manpower of the Axis Powers could no longer support their war effort. The German cities and industries suffered devastating losses but the war effort from the air also cost the Allies a tremendous price. The daylight bombing offensive by the Eighth Air Force cost 4,754 B-17 Flying Fortresses, 2,112 B-24 Liberators, and 2,191 fighter escort-type aircraft lost in combat. Aircrew members numbering 28,000 were killed or missing in action and 28,000 became prisoners of war.

At the end of the war on May 8, 1945, men and equipment were sent home. They returned in their aircraft, 20 men to each four-engine bomber. Altogether, over 4,000 four-engine bombers and 2,000 twin engine planes made the trip back to the U.S. How did such success come in such a short time? Was it leadership, or the equipment, or the men, or fate, or the cause for which they fought?

Their credo: *"Audaces Fortunat juvat timidos que repellit."* "Fortune favors the bold and scorns the timid." Daring young Americans were **bold** beyond measure, but there was more to it than that! There was a prayer base back home in the little villages and cities (some were unaware of it). The names of these brave youth were listed on posters in churches or on signs placed on prominent brick walls in their villages. But more importantly, they were brought before God in prayer on a daily basis. No, it was not by their boldness alone. The Almighty intervened for them. *"So let us come boldly to the throne of our gracious God. There we will receive his mercy, and we will find grace to help us when we need it."(Hebrews 4:16 NLT)* ✞

How About It?

Training for war

KEEPING UP WITH THE TIMES

A few months ago, I bought a new typewriter. It worked differently from the old one. . . but that is no big deal! The problem arose when the ribbon and correction tape was all used up. I arose to the task, went to my dealer, bought replacement ribbons to get back in business but. . .I just couldn't make them fit, the thing just wouldn't work! Somewhat embarrassed, I took the machine and the new ribbons, everything, back to the place where I had bought it. I told the young guy that replacing the ribbon on this new model didn't work like the one I learned on in 1940. In a flash, he popped the new ones in and had it up running again, so simple. As I was leaving the shop I mused aloud, "I wonder how long it will be before someone has to teach me again how to tie my shoes?"

The writer of the Book of Ecclesiastes said, **"there is a right time for everything, a time to be born, a time to die. . .a time to cry and a time to laugh."** Life is a series of events, the pendulum swinging back and forth, no respecter of persons. Things that were once a breeze, situations not too difficult, relationships easy to develop are not as they once were. The writer declares, "**Everything is appropriate in its own time.** "So I conclude that, first, there is nothing better for a man than to be happy and to enjoy

State of the art, 1944

himself as long as he can; and second, that he should eat and drink and enjoy the fruits of his labors, for these are gifts from God." (Ecc.3:1,11-12 NLT) A wise man, that Solomon! ✞

Two old friends were talking:
"I hear that after all of these years
you got married again.
Your new bride must really be a good-looker".
"No, she's not what you might
call attractive looking."
"Well, she must be a good cook".
"No, she doesn't cook much at all".
"Then she must be something else
in the bedroom at night".
"She's not very interested in such as that".
"Well, why did you want to
marry her then?"
"Well you see, I married her because
she can drive at night!".

Deep Discussion

WORTH IT ALL!

I am uncertain when it all began but looking back, it may have started when I was a first grade pupil in a one-room school out on the plains of Oklahoma. Every morning, rain or shine, snow, wind or calm, around 20 rural students formed a circle out in front of the modest white frame building that stood stark and alone on the vastness of its prairie setting. One of the big kids (an eighth grader) presented a folded American flag to a second big kid who attached it to a well-worn cable and solemnly and slowly raised it to the top of the rusty pipe flag pole. With our right hand over our heart, we recited *"I pledge allegiance to the flag of the United States of America."* Miss Wheary had all of her students repeat this pledge every day until the words, their meaning and significance became etched in our memory and hearts. Once inside, we hung up our coats and stocking caps and took our seats and

Celebrating victory in London May 8, 1945, VE Day

bowed our heads while the Bible was read and a prayer was given. Hanging on the wall over the chalk board was the unfinished portrait of the Father of our Nation, George Washington, gazing down upon us. I always felt that he was giving his approval to what we were doing.

How About It?

General Douglas MacArthur, Japanese surrender, August 15, 1945 VJ Day

One of the older kids, the one who conducted the flag-raising ceremony, was Robert Markley. He was a buddy of mine. His dad was a dairy farmer and lived only one mile directly south of our farm. He talked of his desire to be an Air Corps pilot and serve his country. Being seven grades ahead of me, he finished public school, completed his university requirements, enlisted in military service, became a second lieutenant, and earned his silver wings. He was my role model, patriot and idol. Robert became a P-40 fighter pilot assigned to Pearl Harbor.

I had finished high school, was enrolled in university studies and anticipated following the academic and military path that Robert had followed. War erupted. The newspaper headlines reported that the first Oklahoma casualty in the war at Pearl Harbor was Robert Markley, my friend and buddy.
Trotsky made the following statement, *"You may not be interested in war, but war is interested in you!"* Hundreds of thousands of the youth of our country became involved immediately. So did I. This one act only illustrates the basic tenets of our country: freedom, faith, and patriotism. If it is worth enjoying and cherishing, it is worth defending and we did. We exercised faith in our leaders and in our God. We allowed our patriotism to be demonstrated with a renewed commitment to freedom, even when we knew this required personal sacrifice.

At first, the war for the Allies was not going well. Winston Churchill said in a speech, *"We have not journeyed all this way across the centuries, across the oceans, across the mountains, across the prairies, because we are made of sugar candy."* The words of Churchill were true. We were much tougher than our enemies understood. It was costly. The World War II Memorial standing mid–point between the monuments of George Washington and Abraham Lincoln in our Nation's Capital attests to the fact that the war cost many, many lives, but freedom was preserved. The Freedom Wall with its 4,000 gold stars commemorates the more than 400,000 Americans who gave their lives for the cause of freedom. These stars remind me that 280 of them represented 28,000 of my comrades who were lost in the call of duty with the 8th Air Force. One of the earlier stars represented my Oklahoma friend, Robert.

Serving our country is an honor. As I looked at the sea of faces present at the final gathering of our recent Reunion, the faces of the Veterans and their descendents reflected the emotional gratitude, love and pride of freedom they have for our nation, the United States of America. ✞

LOOK AROUND

Two men died. Both were Presidents and leaders of their county. The entire world was informed of this event through the media. The details of their deaths were outlined in the same issues of newspapers and magazines, and were covered simultaneously via world-wide television. One was labeled a *tyrant*. The other was identified as a *healer*. The *tyrant* ruled with a relentless and selfish grip on his people for a quarter of a century. The *healer* served his country for only a few short years. One died on the gallows, the other succumbed to old age. The death of one was recognized with cheers while the news of the other brought tears to the eyes of his countrymen.

Saddam Hussein was considered to be the most notorious dictator of the 20th Century. He was captured, imprisoned, and tried by a Special Iraqi Tribunal composed of five judges. He was charged and found guilty of war crimes, crimes against humanity and genocide. He was sentenced to death by hanging. On 30 December 2006, with his hands bound behind him, he was lead by masked men in leather coats to the gallows. By several accounts, he was calm but scornful of his captors, exchanging taunts and accusations. His last acts of defiance consisted of verbal jousting and silent contempt. The trapdoor upon which he stood snapped open and in a moment, Saddam was dead. The observers in the chamber erupted in shouts… "The tyrant has fallen."

Four days earlier, half a world away, the 38th President of the United States, Gerald Ford died on 26 December 2006. He was a man elected by the people he loved in Michigan and served them as their Representative in Congress. After 8 years as Minority Leader in the House of Representatives, and after a one-of-a-kind series of events, he reportedly said, "A funny thing happened to me on the way to becoming Speaker." The Vice President, Spiro Agnew, after a scandal, resigned office. Gerald Ford was named Vice President. Then President Richard Nixon left the office in disgrace and Ford was elevated to the Presidency, a position he held without having been elected either as Vice President or President. When he died, thousands of ordinary Americans along with many dignitaries came to pay respect to the *Healer*. One speaker in delivering his eulogy remarked: "In our Nation's darkest hour, Gerald Ford lived his finest moment." Another said, "In 1974, America didn't need a philosopher-king or a warrior-prince. We needed a healer, we needed a rock, and we needed honesty and candor and courage. We needed Gerald Ford."

Two extremes: one was self-serving, the other selfless.

In the heat of conflict, Americans have been forged in the truths of democracy and they live and practice these principles. From Bunker Hill to Gettysburg, the Argonne Forest, Iwo Jima and the islands of the Pacific, the air battles over occupied Europe to the war on Terrorism, we have and will continue to pay the price for freedom. Americans of all age groups benefit from what we have in this country - personal freedom, personal choices in determining our destinies, national pride and independence—things for which men and women have fought and died. We have many reasons to be proud.

We must never allow the noisy, vulgar voices of the dissidents among us to cloud or blur the memory of our foundational values that are, as our founding fathers declared, as self-evident: *"Life, liberty and the pursuit of happiness."* King Solomon, thousands of years ago, summarized these same principles when he said: **"Righteousness exalts a nation, but sin is a reproach to any people." (Proverbs 14:34 NKJ)** ✝

How About It?

DEN TOTEN
ZUR EHR
DEN LEBENDEN
ZUR MAHNUNG

**Jewish concentration camp
Memorial, Dachau, Germany**

WHY FEAR?

I have been attacked again! It reminds me of my World War II days when I was making a desperate attempt to get back to England in a crippled bomber from a mission over enemy territory. Our formation would be jumped by a gaggle of angry fighter pilots or else face flak barrages over the target. There were no other choices. We had to contend with one or the other. When there were no fighter planes present, we had to fly through the flak. When there was no flak, the fighters would attack. There was never any question in my mind that the Germans were out to get me one way or another.

Since those days, I have been serenely cruising along and suddenly, I am over seventy years old and I am being attacked again in a variety of other ways. I am getting letters from all of the funeral directors in town volunteering their services, wanting my business, and tombstone salesmen, and retirement or nursing home providers are wanting to "help me out". I can still get life insurance, if I will apply soon! Sounds bleak, but it is true. This is happening to all of us WW II veterans.

Unwittingly, all of the above are peddlers of fear. Their message I already know but a subject that I do not dwell upon very often. Living in fear brings trauma---internal stress prompted by worry. I have friends who start priming their pumps of worry before they get out of bed to view the morning news. Energy is needlessly burned up as the mind runs up and down valleys of uncertainty and dread.

How do we overcome this dilemma? Is seems to me that fear is overcome by trust. We must consciously and willingly abandon ourselves to someone who is trustworthy. It certainly worked for King David, the Biblical leader who said …"**What time I am afraid, I will trust in thee"**. **(Psalms 56:3 KJV)**

The book of Life, that is

Our creator is totally trustworthy. He cares. He is reliable. He isn't unskilled. He isn't out to get us. When we fear, he is saying to us, "This won't hurt a bit, trust me." And he means it! ✝

American Military Cemetery, Madingley Memorial

How About It?

MEMORIES

A noted psychiatrist was addressing a group of aged World War II Veterans on the subject of mental deficiencies. After his address and during the question and answer period that followed, one veteran stood up and asked, "Doc, how do you detect a problem like this in an individual?" "Well," the doctor responded, "he should be able to answer a simple question. If he hesitates, that could be a sign that he has a problem." For example, a question such as "Captain Cook made three trips around the world and died during one of them. Which one?" The veteran, after a short silence, replied with a nervous laugh, "My memory fails me when it comes to history. Could you give me another example?"

What is memory? It is a living diary of everything we experience in a lifetime. It is the recorded accumulation of everything we have learned from birth to death and is a byproduct of our five senses. Something we smell or feel or see brings instant recall of experiences we have had. Memory is what defines our lives. Life without memory is no life at all. Our memory is our connection with the past that also connects us with the realities of today. Memory is our reason, our feeling, even our action for everyday living. Without it, we are lost.

Shakespeare in his play, *As you Like It,* describes the world as a stage with the men and women merely players. He said, "*They have their exits and their entrances, and one man in his time plays many parts.*" He describes seven ages starting with infancy and passing through life, the last being those in their second childhood. Old age is perceived in many different ways but whenever that time comes, God gives us memory so that we can have roses in December. I have been privileged to live a long time and as a consequence, know many others as old or older than I. It is interesting to see how veterans react to their memories. When the memories of some are reverted to the past, films and stories that recall the horrors of battle repulse them. The smell of gunpowder or the sight of a wound and blood drives them away. They are trying to blot out events not of their own choosing and the memories these events bring. Memories linger. We must deal with them.

Our perspective on life must reach beyond ourselves. Our lives and the experiences we have had should not be about the past but about the future. Memories about us, even by our families, will fade but the benefits resulting from our lives will live on and on. The legacy left behind is not to draw attention to our collective memories, but to point to the blessings available to everyone in future generations. The Psalmist in speaking about a good man declared in Psalms, **" Good will come to him who is generous and lends freely, who conducts his affairs with justice. Surely he will never be shaken, a righteous man will be remembered forever. He will have no fear of bad news, his heart is steadfast, trusting in the Lord. His heart is secure, he will have no fear, in the end he will look in triumph on his foes . . .his righteousness endures forever." (Psalms 112:5-8, NIV)** ✝

The Next Generation, keeping connected with the past

SONGS IN THE NIGHT

Our first three day pass! A lot of time had passed and a few combat missions had been flown since we received our Eighth Air Force assignment in England. The coveted reward was announced and my crew and I received advice on how to spend our precious three days away from the base. We considered our options and chose London.

We had received a bird's-eye view of the pastoral scenes of East Anglia from our aircraft and a close-up view when we traveled the country lanes of rural Norfolk. But, we were anxious to get away and experience something different, big city life. The train station in Norwich was bustling and crowded with military personnel of all nationalities and ranks. Mingled in were civilians traveling to who knows where. The quaint passenger train came to a halt, passengers crowded the platform and swarmed the cars seeking a seat. The compartments accommodated eight. The fabric-covered seats were worn and dingy. The windows, covered with a mesh material to prevent shattering, were grimy and almost opaque from soot and the accumulation that came as a result of years of war–time austerity. Mechanically, the train preformed flawlessly and the schedule was kept to perfection. We arrived in London when it was still daylight.

Our destination was the Red Cross Hostel. Our directional questions were asked in Yankee English, and instructions were given in British English. "Piccadilly Circus? You caawnt miss it….it is on Coventry Street, don't you know?" We used various available conveyances, followed the crowd and got there. The Red Cross Hostel was an American oasis. The place sparkled with cleanliness, the women hostesses were beautiful, the beds had clean crisp white linens, the food was food, not chow. And there were suggestions for entertainment. A bulletin board listed places to go, things to do, events galore. The list included Buckingham Palace, the Houses of Parliament, London Bridge, Westminster Abbey and on and on. But, one thing caught my eye! This announcement took precedence over all other things.

The London Philharmonic Orchestra was in concert: Sir Thomas Beecham was the guest conductor! I was just a kid growing up in a small rural, farming community but my talented artistic English born mother and my musical father created in me a love for classical music and I had heard of Royal Albert Hall. This was first on my list.

The darkness didn't deter the cabby we hailed. He threaded his quaint little motor vehicle through the twisted and confusing maze of London's streets. He fought for the space other cabs occupied, and he maneuvered around the multitude of pedestrians stumbling around in the dark streets trying to find their destination. En route to the music hall located on Kensington Gore, wrecked and destroyed buildings littered the streets, thanks to the German bomb's blitz. Sirens were sending out their mournful sounds. Looking eastward, the Brits huge searchlights pierced the night skies searching for enemy aircraft and the flashes of bursting cannon shells were creating quite a show. The cabby remarked, "Well, it looks like Jerry has come to pay another visit to London." We stopped before an imposing structure, Royal Albert Hall. It surprisingly, had been untouched by enemy bombs.

Once past the darkened entrance foyer, the theatre was aglow in light revealing a dazzling architectural marvel. It was filled to capacity with servicemen, dignitaries, and ordinary Brits who were there to enjoy the evening. Already seated on the stage were the musicians with their instruments. Before me, the Royal Philharmonic Orchestra! The house lights dimmed, a hush fell over the assembly, then an explosion of applause when the founder and guest conductor of the Orchestra made his appearance. Tall, stately and dressed impeccably in his black cutaway, Sir Thomas Beecham approached the podium. When he stepped upon the elevated platform, there was absolute silence. Sir Thomas gracefully lifted his arms; the musicians raised their instruments, poised and waiting. When the baton came down, the response was the exhilarating and crashing sound of music coming from the strings, the percussionists, the blaring brass and the woodwinds. The concerted teamwork of a hundred musicians came together for the opening sounds of the overture.

The musicians were mostly women. The few men musicians participating were older. This was wartime England. The women were either widowed or their husbands or boyfriends were serving in the military services. The men, too old to actively serve in the armed forces of His Majesty, the King, were wardens in the Home Guard or some other civilian auxiliary. But they, in this capacity, were serving their King as well. Outside the theatre at that moment, bombs were falling on the city. Searchlights were piercing the darkness trying to locate the intruding aircraft and antiaircraft guns were firing constantly trying to stop them and the carnage they were creating. War was touching the life of every musician and every spectator seated in that place. A war was going on. Every life was being affected. But the music we were hearing was touching and transforming all of our lives. We had witnessed a new song in the night even when there was Hell on the outside and Hell going everywhere around the world.

When the concert ended, the musicians placed their instruments in their cases. The women returned to their bomb-damaged homes, lonely, heartbroken and afraid. The men removed their formal attire and changed to their Warden's uniforms to return to their nightly duty. Spectators went outside into the dark. The world was unchanged. It was the same as when we entered the hall, a chaotic, dirty and dangerous place, but we were different. We had heard a new song that night. Years have passed, but I have never forgotten the beauty of that moment. I was not miraculously delivered from flying combat missions. I returned to East Anglia when my three-day pass ended. I was not then nor have I ever been exempt from the traumas of living in this world, but there was a new song.

Throughout life, our Maker will give us a new song in our darkest nights. An Old Testament character whose name was Job asked the question, **"Where is God my maker who giveth songs in the night?" (Job 35:10 KJV)** Another, David the musician, declared, **"I call to remembrance my song in the night." (Psalm 77:6 NKJ)** If we will only listen, God will give us a new song that we will always remember in its beauty and it will outperform all of the traumas that we will ever experience in life.

Thank God for songs in the night. ✝

DEBRIEFING

Hundreds of American four engine bombers, high in the skies over Germany, were heading eastward. We were the unannounced, unwelcome, and uninvited guests of this warring enemy. Our destination was a synthetic oil refinery. The Allied strategy was to target its transportation system and its petroleum producing capabilities By destroying these, the mobility of their military would be hampered and the end of the war would be hastened. Below, hundreds of flak gunners were determined to stop us. They were firing their cannons desperately into the air and they were having some degree of success. Our aircraft were being hit. Some were targeted and destroyed while others were receiving damage. Airmen attempting to survive were leaving their crippled aircraft. White parachutes billowed out and were floating down in a sky filled with black, greasy, flashing shell bursts. Many of the chutes were open but some had men who were hanging helplessly beneath a tangled mess of straps and chords. Some were burning. They were our friends and buddies. Looking downward we saw the results of our bombing, hundreds of vivid flashes of bomb bursts mixed in with dirt and the twisted metal structures of a seriously destroyed oil refinery. Shooting upward were oily and billowing black clouds mingled with leaping flames. There was utter confusion, chaos and destruction.

Our damaged formation of planes droned on and on. It seemed to us like an eternity before we were finally back home and safe on the ground. All of our crew was still alive; our aircraft was damaged but was still intact. Some of the aircraft and men were not as fortunate! At our revetment, the engines were shut down, we deplaned, and our usual brief critique with our faithful ground crew was completed. We got on board the waiting GI truck and headed to the headquarters building.

Returning crews, somber, fatigued and anxious, filled the large smoke-filled room. Coffee, donuts and sandwiches were available for the men. There was a long wait before a table became available, ten chairs for the crew, another for the intelligence officer. An enlisted man brought a tray of ten small glasses full of booze, the pilot signed for it and the members of the crew quickly consumed them. The debriefing began. What happened? When? Where? What did you see? On and on the interrogation proceeded until the officer was certain he had gleaned everything he could about the mission experience from the tired men. They were dismissed to turn in their flight gear and head for the chow hall. The reports were sent off to Headquarters.

The debriefing information was vital to the men who would fly tomorrow's mission. What information about the mission flown today would help in the missions to be flown in the future? What could be learned? What could they expect in the future? This was the procedure used sixty years ago by the men of World War II. We are now a rapidly vanishing generation. What useful information have we learned which, if passed on, would be useful for those following us?

Living these years, we have been shaped and influenced by everything we have experienced. We have mingled with all kinds of people. When those who have beliefs and values that are like ours, we have harmony but when there is a differing of opinions, goals and objectives and how to achieve them, there is conflict. How we handle conflict shows the kind of person we really are. Our society is full of individuals whose situations we often shun or ignore. Thinking about them brings us emotional conflict. How do we respond to gays or lesbians, divorced, handicapped, unemployed or perpetual welfare recipients? We have communities full of illegal immigrants, centers for the addicted and homes for the mentally and physically handicapped. Our jails and penitentiaries are full of criminals who are misfits in society. There are street gangs in ever increasing numbers. We have terrorists, those who speak out against democracy, and those who freely receive the benefits of our great country but are indifferent or openly oppose the principles upon which our country was founded. These are but a sampling of the many conflicts we encounter. The big question is "How have we learned to deal with them?" Some try to ignore them. Often, our fear of doing the wrong thing prevents us from doing anything. We must keep in mind that these conflicts are caused by people who feel rejected. They are in need of a godly and compassionate touch. Our own character is revealed by how we deal with these everyday conflicts.

Someone has wisely said that *character is that quality of our life that we have when we are in a dark and solitary place when no one is looking*. It is that characteristic that is hidden but is eventually revealed and seen by the eyes of the public. Tom Landry, an 8th Air Force World War II B-17 pilot, demonstrated a high profile example of character in his civilian life. During his wartime years, he was a member of the 493rd BG known as Helton's Hellcats and flew thirty-five bombing missions in the European Theatre of Operations. As a civilian, he became the legendary and much loved coach of the Dallas Cowboy and served them for twenty-nine years. The team changed ownership, a new coach was named and immediately Tom Landry, much to the disbelief and dismay of his admiring public, was fired. His true character came out. Joe Gibbs, former coach of the Washington Redskins and one of his colleagues said: *"It wasn't his wins or losses, but rather the kind of person he was. Tom was a great moral person and led a lot of people to Christ."* In his leadership role, there were many crises but he was a man of moral courage and undeniable character.

To what then do we attribute the building of character? Why do some generations seem to have more of it than others? Could it be that "the lap of luxury or ease of living or lack of convictions or a lack of purpose in living" do not foster strong character? As exercise contributes to muscle development, conflict and stress strengthens one's character. "Grow up or fold up" was the philosophy of our generation when we were young. Face life as it is dealt you. Don't run away! Stand up for what is right. We stood strong. Character and courage were fostered. We are not given a lifetime supply of courage to draw upon. We are always expending it. Life and living have taught us that there is a source of replenishing and we must tap into it! The writer of Psalms gave us the secret, **"Wait on the Lord: be of good courage, and he will strengthen our heart." (Psalms 27:14 KJV)**

A physician had, across the years of his practice, been privileged to share the most profound time in the lives of his patients, including their feelings during their final moments on earth. He observed that in those moments, the dying do not think about the degrees they earned in college, what positions they held, or how much wealth they had accumulated. At the end, he declares, what really matters is whom you love and who loved you. He concluded this to be a good measure of the success of one's life. St. Paul the Apostle faced many crises throughout his life, the greatest being when he was awaiting his own execution He declared, **"I have fought a good fight, I have finished my course, I have the faith." (II Timothy 4:7 KJV)** And likewise, when we face our final moments, we can sit down and chat with the Great Interrogator. Hopefully He will say, "You did well. Come on in." ✝

How About It?

QUOTES AND NOTES

The quotations cited in these essays come from a variety of sources: from literature, from interviews, from the Internet, from casual conversations with the Veterans, from speeches, which I have heard across the years. I have made notes from many of these and used them freely. This was never intended to be a scholarly or research manual. When each article was written, no attempt was made to document each source in a bibliographic or academic format. Instead, I am giving credit by listing the individuals in alphabetic order with number(s) following each name, citing the page in which the quotation is given.

Scriptural citations are from the Holy Bible and have been taken from four versions: (1) the <u>King James Version</u> (KJV); (2) the *New King James Version* (NKJV); (3) the *New International Version* (NIV); and (4) the *New Living Translation* (NLT).